becoming her

becoming her

Kayleigh Payne-Gary

God

MANIFEST | PUBLISHING
www.GodManifestPublishing.com

This book and all other God Manifest Publishing books are available on Amazon.com.

Cover designed by Jonnathan Zin Truong
Interior designed by Uyen Vu

For more information on foreign distributors, email
publishers@godmanifestpublishing.com
Reach us at on the internet: www.godmanifestpublishing.com

ISBN: 979-8-9920028-3-6
eBook: ISBN: 979-8-9920028-4-3

Printed in the United States of America.

TABLE OF CONTENTS

TABLE OF CONTENTS

PROLOGUE

I have written the first few pages of this book many times. It has been on my heart for many years to write. However, every time I set down to get started, I find that I am at a loss for words. It is very uncommon for me to be at a loss for words. It is a known fact that women speak approximately 20,000 words a day; somehow, I think I say double that. At least, that is what my close friends and family say. For me to be at a loss for words is simply rare. Yet, here I am, trying to formulate the many thoughts and ideas I have into a format that others will not just read but also enjoy reading. I have spent time in prayer, spent time in thought, and spent a lot of time in excitement and with others. "What should I write about?" "Who will my audience be?" "I feel passionate about marriage and the family unit, but I have only been married for six years. Certainly, no one would want to read a book about marriage from a *twenty-something*." I wondered if I should just tell my story. But I have so many stories that I was unsure which ones should be told. Would anyone be interested in hearing my stories? Which parts of myself am I vulnerable enough to share?

For months or even years, I would start to write, then stop. I would decide I was not good enough or talented enough to write a book. I would convince myself that no one would care what God was doing in me or through me, and it did not need to be shared. I would go on a binge of doing absolutely nothing—well mostly nothing; social media and online shopping were there to keep me plenty busy—and then I would pray. God would reinspire me to write. I would pick up the iPad, iPhone, MacBook, or whatever device was handy at the time and equipped with Google Docs, and I would write. I would get a few pages in, Google how many pages the average book should be, and convince myself that I was not capable of formatting the things God was showing me into written chapters. And then I would delete the whole thing. This process would continue repeatedly until one day, driving home, after a weekend filled with family and friends bringing in the New Year together. I looked at my husband; he was driving our silver 2015 Toyota Camry, focused on the road ahead of him. We were talking; I was talking, leaving no room for empty air. And I asked him this, "Why do people say that they can listen to me talk all day?" He responded, "Who said that?"

I answered his question in true Kayleigh fashion—by word-vomiting on him. "Well, this girl, Alyssa, told me that at a retreat I was speaking at. Karen told me at her Bible study one night that she loved to hear me tell stories, and Abbie and Maegan told me the other night that they couldn't imagine why I was ever insecure about being in the friend group, because I belong there, and I make anything fun, and I can tell any story well." As Donovan formed his words to answer my question, I continued, "I just do not see myself as someone who people feel like they can listen to. I most of the time feel insecure, like I do not have anything to offer, so I genuinely do not understand why they said that to me."

> *Out of the abundance of the heart,*
> *The mouth speaks."*
> **MATTHEW 12:34 (ESV)**

It was true. Out of the abundance of my insecurities and negative self-talk that were ever-so-present in my heart came a genuine statement out of my mouth. I do not have anything to offer. My favorite singer/songwriter, Taylor Swift, wrote a song that says these words: "Actually, I always felt I must look better in the rearview." Those words perfectly depict how I feel most of the time, or at least how I feel as I type words onto this page. Sit down. You are talking too much. They do not care what you have to say. Do not push yourself to the forefront. Be quiet. You are too disorganized to be anointed. I feel like I am too much while also consistently feeling I am too little most of the time; I felt exactly that way as I was asking Donovan why people were complimenting me. Donovan responded, "Kayleigh, they are saying you are a good communicator. When you are settled on what you think about something, you have a knack for communicating how you feel in a way that people can relate to."

I pondered his response for hours after this conversation. How do everyone and anyone see me as a good communicator and storyteller—a way that I certainly cannot see myself? Surely this is not only a feeling that I struggle with. I cannot be the only woman who is confident that she is called, chosen, and purposed to do remarkable things for the Kingdom of God while constantly being so uncertain of her ability to step into all that God has called her to. In pondering his response, I started writing. At the time I started writing this book, I did not have a title for my book… heck, I did not even know it was going to be a book. I thought it was going to be a long journal entry, maybe a blog post broken up into parts, but it seems like God had other plans. Since you are reading this, you know that this is a book titled *Becoming Her*. The insecurities I have about my own purpose and destiny are what shaped these pages, and what I hope makes this book relatable to you. I believe that, as people, we are all becoming something— as believers, we are all on a journey to becoming the people God created us to be—the best versions of ourselves. As women, we are all on our way to becoming the version of us that is not insecure, timid, or scared of our purpose. We are on our way to becoming HER. At least, I am. And I pray that, if you are not on your journey to becoming the woman that God has created you to be, you will find yourself somewhere in these chapters as we journey through my adventure to become her together.

Chapter 1

YOU HAVE NOTHING TO OFFER

I was born in 1994 to the greatest family. My grandparents spoiled me as often as they could; my aunts and uncles loved me like I belonged to them; and my parents would have died trying to give my brother and me the best life. I lived in a quiet, quaint neighborhood. I lived on a road with no lines in the middle of it—the kind where kids and animals could frolic in the street without their parents fearing they would get run over. We spent summers playing cops and robbers until the streetlights came on. My neighbors' parents would signal them to come in for dinner by blowing a whistle loud enough for us all to hear. The whistle was the signal for them to come inside, but once that whistle blew, the whole neighborhood went in for the night.

My backyard had a swing set, a pool, and a sandbox. When I was younger, all of my birthday parties were pool parties. It was a free venue, and all my friends enjoyed having contests to determine who could make the biggest splash and who could eat their popsicles the quickest. In true nineties fashion, all the neighborhood kids— my brother and myself included—owned a pair of those skater shoes. It was years before the popular shoe Heelys was a brand, and unlike Heelys, these shoes did not have one wheel on the heel. We just called these shoes "skate shoes," and with the push of a button, four wheels would pop out of the bottom of your shoe, and you went from having tennis shoes to having actual skates. I recall one winter when my parents did not tarp up our pool. It was cold enough outside that the pool had frozen over, but the temperature did not stop us from playing outside. My brother and I had the bright idea to go ice-skating with our skate shoes on the frozen pool. While nothing terrible happened, although the scenarios were endless, my mom freaked out and made us come inside. As we grew older, we lost interest in swimming. Eventually, my parents took the pool down, but that still did not stop us from enjoying the life our parents had built for us. I was saved at an early age; I went to church almost as much as I went to school, and I learned to hear God and started to practice prophesying in middle school. Despite the drama and heartbreaks that occurred in high school and the parties and freedoms that college offered, I never strayed from the foundation of Christ that my family had laid for me.

As I journeyed through my young adult life, God began to awaken this calling in me to preach. I can remember preaching my first sermon to a group of adults in the "big church." I had spent hours preparing, days reading over notes, compiling scriptures, and remembering stories to tell that went along with the words God had laid on my heart. As my uncle/pastor announced my name and called me to the stage, I had that same feeling in my gut that I had when I was playing flag football at the city park with the neighborhood boys when I was in the third grade. The football went flying through the air; I went running to chase it, and I definitely caught it, right in the gut! I fell to the grass with my breath knocked out of me. However, this time, no one threw a football or hit me in the gut. The sound of the floor squeaking underneath my heavy footsteps as I walked to the stage was enough to take my breath away, and as my breath left my body, my mind took off with it. The sermon that took me days to prepare took me mere minutes to preach, and the only thing I can remember from that sermon were the words: "I would swerve to miss a butterfly." I wish I had saved sermon notes so that I could remind myself why those words rolled off of my tongue, but they are long gone—much like my breath was as I stepped toward the purple, carpeted stage.

There was a small crowd that filled the mint green chairs that Sunday night, and after my five-minute sermon, the ladies who attended that church for many years told me that I "did such a good job," but they could not have been telling the truth. My insecurities were met with certainties when one of the ladies smiled at me as she left and told me "not to hit any butterflies on the way home." I could not help but smile, as I knew her comment meant no harm. She was trying to encourage me in a joking manner, but still, my insecurities were affirmed. I look back on that night, and although I was not offended by the comments and compliments that seemed forced, I remember feeling like I did not have anything to offer. My story was not one that told of Jesus saving me from addiction. I had never even smelled weed until my first year of marriage, and that was because my neighbors used to smoke it in our small apartment complex. I do not have a story of growing up in an abusive home. I was not sneaking out, egging cars, or teepeeing surrounding neighborhoods with my friends. I have a testimony of being saved at an early age and never straying from the truth of what was. Surely no one could relate to that.

> *"... Her sins, which are many, are forgiven—*
> *for she loved much,*
> *But he who is forgiven little loves little."*
> **LUKE 7:47 (ESV)**

I recall that late in my dating relationship, my now husband and I had attended his church on a Wednesday night, and the pastor was sharing the story of a sinful woman that was featured in Luke 7. During the story, he paused and asked a lady in the audience, "Why do you love Jesus so much?" She responded, "Because He loves me so much." She continued, "If I told you all of the things I have been through in my life, the things Jesus saved me from and brought me through, you would not have even asked me that." The pastor responded, "You love much because you were forgiven much."

In an instant, insecurities that I had spent several years laying to rest crept back, and my mind raced. Surely, I could never tell others about the love of Jesus; perhaps I had never even experienced it.

People in the Christian world often say, "Jesus loved me back to life," but I was already living. I was young, naive, spoiled by my parents, and engaged to a good man; I believed that I could do anything, be anybody, and life was going great—exactly how my thirteen-year-old self imagined it would be. Maybe I had been forgiven little, and my love for Jesus was little as a result.

> *"Before I shaped you in the womb,*
> *I knew all about you.*
> *Before you saw the light of day,*
> *I had holy plans for you..."*
> **JEREMIAH 1:5 (MSG)**

I cringe even to type those words. Several years later, I am on the other side of that insecurity—not that I do not have others I struggle with. I wish I could hug my twenty-one-year-old self and inform her of the things I know now. I wish I could tell her that the testimony of being captivated by Jesus at an early age and never losing your wonder of Him is an amazing testimony. I wish I could tell her that, even though the world thinks she does not have much to offer because she has never been through anything, they are grossly wrong. She will go through heartbreaking seasons that will leave her depressed and defeated, but her closeness to and wonder of God will steady her, and her story will impact people. I wish I could tell her that before she was formed in her mother's womb, Jesus knew what she would be like. He knew she would be loud. He knew she would love too hard and trust too easily. He knew she would be insecure, that she would wish she were prettier and smarter. He knew she would wish to be like the other girls her age. Elegant and neat—presentable. I wish I could tell her that regardless of every insecurity and angst she had regarding herself, Jesus loves her fiercely, wholly, and completely. I would inform her that, despite all of her insecurities, Jesus ONLY wants her to know, love, and trust Him.

One of my favorite things to do is to drive around and listen to Taylor Swift—to be alone with myself, my thoughts, and my music. Occasionally, I will bring someone else into that, asking them to ride around with me. One particular night, one of my best friends was home visiting from college, and I had asked her to ride around town with me. When you live in a small town, riding around is the best pastime. We drove through neighborhoods casually yelling the words to song lyrics, but slowly the radio faded, and conversation about how college—how life—was going took its place. My friend informed me then, and has mentioned it several times since then, that the biggest, and perhaps the most freeing takeaway from her freshman year of college was that, more than Jesus wanted to use her to reach people, He wanted to love her.

What I know now that I did not realize then is that our main goal as Christians is not to share Him with others. This is a controversial statement, and many may disagree, but let me explain. So many leaders in Christian culture preach "find your calling" and "step into your purpose." It leaves young people, like myself, believing that the whole reason they are alive is to do something. We fantasize about what it will be like when we finally step into our callings. Will people know us, will they validate us, affirm us, tell us how talented or gifted we are, and how anointed we are? This is a slippery slope; if we are not careful, we get so caught up in what we are doing that we lose sight of who we were doing it for in the first place. We lose the identity that Jesus gives us and pick the one that society gives us.

My sweet friend helped me to see that our purpose as believers is to have a relationship with Christ—to know, to love, and to trust God. Philippians 3:8 tells us that everything is worthless when compared to the intimate value of knowing Christ. Why does it matter that I share His word eloquently or prophesy accurately if I have failed to know the One who gifted me to do those things? I did not believe it at twenty-one, but I have never been more convinced at twenty-nine that I would give up everything I was "called" to do to better know the One who called me to do it. In Luke 10, an expert in religion comes to Jesus and asks Him how he can inherit eternal life. Amazingly, Jesus' answer was not to go into the city and preach a word; it was not to go and start laying hands on the blind. The answer Jesus gave was simple: "Love the Lord your God with all your heart, soul, and your might. Then you will inherit eternal life." This scripture on its own validates our purpose—to love God with every fiber of our being. Proverbs 3:5 tells us to trust in the Lord and not to lean on our own understanding and He will make our paths straight.

I do not say these things to take away from our calling, as purpose and callings are different. Our purpose is to know, love, and trust Christ, but it is out of our affection for Him that we serve Him. In service to God is where we find callings—preaching, worship leading, and being involved in kids' church. I say these things only to annotate the struggles I encountered from my late teens into early adulthood. I was so focused on serving God, riddled with anxiety, and the fear that I had nothing to offer the Kingdom. I found over time that I was offering the wrong things. I was offering my service, but not my affection; my giftings, but never my devotion. Perhaps the girl who felt as if she had nothing to offer was offering the wrong things, and the girl who thought that her story was invalid because her past was not "rocky" enough would realize that Jesus WAS writing a story that testified to the grace and mercy of the Father.

A FAIRY TALE WEDDING

It was a Sunday morning, chilly outside, but not cold. It was October 16th, 2016. It was my wedding day. I was finally getting ready to marry the man that I had loved for nearly four years. I remember the days leading up to the wedding. I recall sitting on brown barstools in my childhood home with my maid of honor, all of my bridesmaids, and my best friend's mom. I can still hear the giggling as we reminisced and folded fans that would be wedding favors for our guests. I recall the anxiety I felt in my stomach when I realized that my spray tan did not fade like it was supposed to and that I would likely be orange at my wedding. My best friend's mom doused me with peroxide, hoping to take away some of the orange color. I am still so thankful that it worked. Kind of. I definitely had orange armpits on our honeymoon. I remember leaving my mom's house that night after we finished making the wedding favors to sleep in my apartment for the first time with all of my bridesmaids. It was surreal to know that by the end of the following day, I was going to be a wife. The feeling, although surreal, was also calming. I knew that my soon-to-be husband was the one that God had for me. He was kind and gentle. He was chasing after what God had for him. He was everything I had prayed for.

The wedding day was the most perfect day. The morning of the wedding, my friends and I drove to my mother's home to get some last-minute decorations we had left there the night before. My bridesmaids and I all wore matching button-downs with our initials monogrammed on them. Of course, my button-down was white, and it featured navy blue lettering; theirs were blush pink with navy blue lettering. We had monogrammed cups to sip water out of as we were getting our hair and makeup done. My sweet bridesmaid, who doubled as a photographer, took some photos and selfies of us getting ready before arriving at the venue; I still treasure those photos. The ladies who completed my hair and makeup made me look and feel like a Barbie doll. I recall looking at myself in the mirror for the first time after I had finished getting ready. I was standing in a private room with only two of my bridesmaids next to me. I stated, "This is the first time I have looked at myself today! I am so pretty!" I often find myself feeling insecure about how I look, but I certainly was not that day. I felt like I looked like a princess.

As the day progressed, it seemed like it continued to get sweeter. At one point in the afternoon, before it was time to walk down the aisle, my husband and I met on the corner of the upstairs balcony to have a time of prayer together. He stood on one corner and I on the other, and with only the edge of the building between us, my soon-to-be husband interlocked his fingers with mine and led us in a prayer. I had been told by my family and friends that it was bad luck to see your soon-to-be spouse before you walked down the aisle, but that did not stop me from sneaking a peek at him. He was so handsome standing there, eyes closed, and head bowed. My fluffy, champagne-colored dress on my fair skin was perfectly accented by his navy blue tux and dark skin. We were a perfect match.

Finally, the moment arrived to walk down the aisle. My dad walked me down the aisle to the sound of my father-in-law singing "When I First Saw You" by Jamie Fox. My dad, who still denies it, was crying as he walked me down the aisle, but I was beaming from ear to ear with pride to be marrying the man I had loved for nearly four years. My precious uncle officiated our wedding ceremony; he grinned with joy as he led Donovan and me in communion, and again, as he announced us as man and wife. Our whole wedding party danced away from the altar, after we took a selfie with a hot pink selfie stick, to Donovan's newly released single "World Can't Hold Us." The night ended with us dancing, having cake and sparkling grape juice, eating leftovers from the buffet, taking photos with friends and family, and a sparkler sendoff—truly the best day ever. I recall not crying the entire day, except when people were leaving. I was so sad that the most perfect day had come to a close.

My uncle, who officiated our wedding with tears in his eyes, always says after officiating any wedding, "Today the wedding, every day after today, the marriage." The days after our wedding were great. Our honeymoon was filled with days at Disney World and Busch Gardens. We visited the beach and downtown Orlando. Even the drive home from Florida that featured busted tires in rural Georgia was fun. If the honeymoon was an indicator of how blissful marriage would be, we were certainly on the right track. After the honeymoon, we returned home very zealous. I cannot speak for Donovan and what kind of husband he thought he would be in those early years, but I had this dream of being the kind of wife I wished to be. I wanted to be the one who always kept a tidy, clean home—the one with the nicely labeled organizers in the cabinets and pantry. I wanted to be the wife who made sure that the clothes were always clean, dinner was always on the table by 5.30 p.m., and by 9 p.m., my husband's lunch was packed and placed in the refrigerator for him to grab on his way to work the next day. I dreamed about how we would be a couple who did not fight because we were both great communicators. I fantasized about "not going to bed mad" and thought that marriage would be like a sleepover with your best friend every single night.

I am not the only person I had expectations for. While I was going to be the perfect wife, Donovan was going to be the perfect husband. He would make sure that we never struggled with money, he would be the one to take the trash out; it would never be me. I thought we would eat dinner together every night, that Donovan would be the perfect leader, the best communicator, and that he would always listen to me. *I had it all planned out!*

Chapter

2

A NIGHTMARE MARRIAGE

Every expectation that I had set for myself and for Donovan had dissipated by month three; by month six, those expectations had become mere disappointments. I wanted to wash and fold several loads of laundry a day—really, I did—but our apartment did not have connections for a washer and dryer, and I was far too busy with work and my last semester of college to go to the laundromat. I wanted to have lunches prepared for Donovan daily and dinner cooked nightly, but I was a server and still enrolled in college—what was the bother with eating out several nights (every night) a week? I just knew that Donovan and I were excellent communicators but, gosh, he just never listened to me. And while Donovan did have good leadership skills, he just needed constant redirection from his wife.

Do not be deceived by the previous paragraph, which is tinged with a bit of sarcasm, and think a breakdown in communication was our biggest issue. We were facing much more than "you did not wash the dishes" and "you are not communicating well." I stated in the previous paragraph that I was too busy with my senior year of college to fold laundry every day—that is not me being dramatic. I skipped class to go on a honeymoon, and when I got back home, I had to jump right back into the swing of things in order to ensure that I passed my classes so that I could graduate in December. My college was an hour and a half away from where we were living, so I found myself spending a lot of time on the road, driving to and from class. To give perspective, I put about thirty thousand miles on my new car in less than a year. The average American puts thirteen thousand miles on their car every year. This would not have been an issue, except that we only had one car. Just a few weeks before our wedding, Donovan's car died. This car was going to cost thousands of dollars to fix, which we could not afford, and we definitely could not afford a new one while we were trying to pay for a wedding, so we decided to sell the car for scrap metal. We thought it would be best to be a single-car family for a period of time.

The burden of having one car put an even further strain on our marriage when Donovan, otherwise known as DonReady, chose to coach basketball on top of being out of town every weekend for a concert for his music career. Arguments about who was taking the car usually ended with me going to basketball games I did not care about and concerts I was not in support of. It is not that I did not want Donovan to coach basketball or attend concerts for his music; he loved those things. It was just that at this point in our marriage we had been married for six months, and aside from two to three Saturdays that were set aside for my college graduation and a celebratory trip to Disney World, the rest were spent out of town at a ballgame or concert—all things that Donovan either wanted to do or felt like he had to do. On many days, we would spend our Saturday mornings at a ballgame and our Saturday nights at a concert. Due to having one car, I felt forced to always be at the games and events. I mean, really, what other options did I have? I suppose I could have stayed in my small, one-bedroom apartment all day. Alone. I felt as if I was never getting to spend any weekends doing anything that I personally enjoyed, and although he and I were spending time together on the weekends going to ballgames and events, we were not really doing anything we both enjoyed together—there was no team building. There were only two people living two separate lives, but under the covenant of marriage. There was no unity.

Also, not only was I disappointed that my marriage was lacking unity, but I was really missing spending time with my mother/ best friend. Up until I got married, we did everything together. I also began to feel as if all of my time was being spent fueling only Donovan's passions. What about the things I was passionate about? I know that I was insecure, but I wanted to be used by God, too—what about my dreams? As time went on without much change in our weekly agenda, joy became a facade. I felt like the man I married had no time for me and was not caring enough to be available for me. I felt like my goals, dreams, passions, and desires were nominal compared to the things Donovan had going on. I had become convinced that I was unwanted; my feelings and insecurities told me my dreams were invalid, and I was feeling like I was better off having not gotten married at all.

As if time spent was not a big enough issue, money became an issue. In my junior year of college, I made the mistake of signing two apartment leases, thinking that I would be able to get out of one before the other one started. I was wrong. In order to pay both rents, I was forced to take out credit cards. In that year of college alone, I managed to rack up over four thousand dollars in credit card debt just to pay my living expenses. This did not count the places where I also had in-store credit cards. My husband inherited a lot of debt on the day he said, "I do," and I take full responsibility for that. However, the credit card debt did not stop there. Due to Donovan coaching basketball and doing music, he had to cut back on shifts at work. I was already not working much because of school. Despite both of us cutting our work hours back, the bills still had to be paid. And the credit card debt just kept piling up.

I hate to speak of how little money we had without shedding some light on the severity of the situation, so let me do that. During this season, I completely stopped taking my thyroid medicine. It was only thirty dollars a month, but that was much more than I could afford. As a result of that, I gained nearly thirty pounds. On our first and second Christmases as a married couple, we did not put up a Christmas tree because we could not afford one. And even if we could have, we could not have afforded decorations, too. Once, I recall baking my mom a cake for her birthday. I was not able to buy her a gift, but she deserved something. It was not all bad, though. God certainly showed up for us, making a way when there truly was no way.

There was a specific Wednesday when it became evident that we serve a God who makes a way when there is not one. On Wednesdays, our routine was the same. Donovan was the youth leader at church, so we had to get there early. On this particular Wednesday, my car's gas tank was empty, and we did not have groceries in our home. With $5 in our pocket, we had a choice to make. Do we get gas and go to church, or do we skip church and go get some ramen noodles for dinner? As I was contemplating what we would do, I felt like I heard the Lord say, "Check the mailbox." As believers, we pray at least every Sunday for checks in the mail, gifts, surprises, and all sorts of things when we tithe. When I heard the Lord say to check the mailbox, I was certain that someone had sent a check. I was wrong. Our mailbox was a few minutes' walk from our apartment, and because of that, we only checked the mail once a week, if that. When I got to the mailbox, I turned the key, and envelopes fell out of the mailbox from having not checked the mail for several days. One envelope that fell out was actually not an envelope at all. It was an ad for Watermark Toyota. This ad had a key glued to it, and the words next to the key said this: "Bring this key to our dealership to try to start THIS 2018 vehicle." Underneath the words and the key was a photo of a very nice, yellow, sporty-looking car.

Having been certain that I heard the voice of God to check the mail, I was sure that Donovan and I would go to the Toyota dealership and find that we had the magic key. We were going to win that vehicle. If you know anything about new vehicles, the dealership fills them up for you with gasoline. This would mean that I would not have to choose between church and dinner! I would be arriving at church in a brand-new car with a full tank of gas. Despite my expectations, I was wrong. However, just for bringing in the key and attempting to start the vehicle, the dealership gave us five dollars. Although it was not a car, these five dollars were an answer to prayer. We would be able to put five dollars in the gas tank and spend five dollars at Kroger on some ramen. We would not have to choose! Even though God provided for us financially on multiple occasions, the strain on our marriage continued to worsen. Because of how neglected I felt as a wife, I started to develop this general disdain for Donovan. I was always rude to him, never supportive of his music, and anytime he wanted to do anything extra—anything other than what I viewed as the necessities—I acted insane. No, *really*. Once, when Donovan was going to a concert, the morning had been filled with arguing. I, feeling neglected, of course, did not want him to go. After an intense argument that consisted of me yelling things like "You are never here for me" and "You do not care about me," I began *taking his music equipment out of his car and dragging it up the stairs.*

On another occasion, I was cooking spaghetti. It was Donovan's favorite food, and we rarely had much money to eat things we really enjoyed, so this was a treat. I was struggling with depression at this point, and even getting out of bed was a task. Cooking dinner? That was like running a marathon. I had stayed home from work on this day; I did not work much at all, really, and I was proud of myself for getting out of bed and cooking Donovan his favorite meal. When Donovan walked in the door, he did not greet me with the welcoming "Thank you" I had expected. His words rolled off of his tongue like ice. "Making spaghetti is the only thing you did today?" he asked as he scooped the last serving of spaghetti onto his plate. I rebutted with an excuse about how I felt all day and how this was a task because my mental health was struggling. Still, he continued to fill the room with sharp words that cut like a knife. In an instant, I walked over to his plate and picked up his spaghetti—not his plate, his actual spaghetti noodles—fork and all with my hands. I walked it over to the trash, threw it away, and went to the kitchen sink to wash the sauce off my hands. I went into the bedroom and plopped down on the bed as if nothing had happened. Donovan, livid, left the house to get dinner from elsewhere. Although I was satisfied with my pettiness and my ability to make Donovan as angry with me in a moment as I was most of the time with him, I knew that I was wrong. My mental health was depleted. I was depressed and anxious; I probably would have been diagnosed with other mental health disorders had I gone to therapy in that season of my life. My emotions were running me.

Still, knowing that I was wrong did not change my behavior. I engaged in some very erratic behavior—things I would be embarrassed to share publicly. For almost three years, the walls of our home were filled with anger, a lack of intimacy, a ton of arguing, and, sometimes, absolute insanity. I often say, "I did not know that I was crazy until I got married," and while my insanity was a cry for help and a cry for attention, it only pushed Donovan farther away. He coached more basketball teams. He made more music, did more shows, and got more involved with church. No one knew that our home was full of bitterness, anger, arguing, and a lack of intimacy. At least, they have not yet.

I am the kind of person who wears her heart on her sleeve. My husband tells me often that one of my best traits is how genuine I am. I am often told that I am blunt and very forward. If my mouth does not tell you how I feel, usually my facial expressions will. I am not mean, but I do not typically leave things unsaid. While I have learned over the years to speak less, say things with more grace, and be less blunt, I have not yet achieved the practice of consistently speaking with grace and tact. I am working on it and do strive to be better; however, during the first few years of marriage, I was not working on it. I was not striving to be better, and the disdain I had for my spouse crept out of the crevices of my home and into the open space of everyday life.

I recall one night when I called my absolute best friend to ask if she wanted to drive around. Without hesitation, she said yes, and

I told her she would have to come pick me up because we had one car and Donovan was at basketball practice. My friend agreed, and within minutes we were driving around our small town, chatting about life. Due to me being a newlywed, "How is everything going?" was a common question. When my sweet friend asked me in the car how I was doing, it was as if someone had pressed the release button that was hidden on the inside of my heart. As tears streamed down my face, words spewed out of my mouth. I was finally being honest with someone about how I was struggling with my marriage. In the climax of the conversation, my sweet friend said, "Why did you not tell me?" to which I responded, "How do you tell people that you hate the man you married?"

At that moment, I realized that hate was the only emotion I had felt toward Donovan for many months, but up until that point, no one other than Donovan knew what I was feeling. Looking back on the situation, I realize that I mostly kept it secret out of shame. I had gone into marriage so confident that things would be peachy. How do I tell my dad that the man he gave me away to does not even answer the phone when I call him? How do I tell my mama that I miss home and regret getting married? How do I tell my uncle/the pastor who officiated our wedding, who has never even uttered the "D" word (divorce) in his home, that I have gone as far as sitting in the County Clerk's office parking lot debating if I should go in to get divorce papers? Perhaps the only reason I did not go in to get them was out of fear that I would see someone I knew in there. After all, we do live in a small town, and word travels fast when there is gossip to be told. Had I seen someone I knew in the clerk's office, it would have taken approximately three hours for the entire town to know my marriage was failing.

Despite my shameful efforts to prevent people from realizing how bad our marriage really was, people began to figure it out when my disdain for him became public. On our first-year anniversary, I posted something on Instagram to commemorate our eating of the first layer of our wedding cake. The post said something like "Sometimes I wanted to punch you, and sometimes I wanted to punch the walls." This was the first time I had ever been publicly open about how I was struggling in my marriage, but if my Instagram did not tell you, my actions sure would have. I began to be publicly disrespectful to Donovan. Once, Donovan was coaching his brother's basketball team in Bowling Green, KY. In Bowling Green, there was a restaurant that we both loved to eat at called Shoguns. It was a restaurant that we frequently visited when we were dating. The food and atmosphere were great, and it was cheaper at lunchtime. Knowing we were going to a tournament that was going to take up most of our day, I asked before our arrival at the gym if we could eat lunch there during the break period when the team was not playing. Donovan said yes, but like many of his promises in that season, it went unmet when Donovan decided he wanted to skip lunch and watch the rest of the teams play so he could see who his competition would be in the next game. While this in and of itself would not have been a big deal, our marriage was already on the rocks because I felt like my wants and needs were going unmet in many areas.

I started to argue with Donovan, loud enough for others to hear, and while I cannot remember my exact words to him, I am sure it went something like this: "You never do what you say; you always make sure you have time for basketball and writing songs that no one listens to, but you never make sure you keep your word to me." I would pause, Donovan would say nothing, and then I would continue, "And why do you need to watch the other team anyway? You already know what their strengths and weaknesses are. This is not the first tournament with this same group of kids we have been to." Donovan would say nothing, and I would continue, "And I do not understand why you are even coaching this team anyway; I begged you not to, and you did not care. It is not a big deal to get freaking lunch." Heads would turn to see the commotion; I would make eye contact, and they would look away, but their ears were still focused on the eruption of bitterness that I was spewing.

Although Donovan did end up taking me to lunch, it was not enjoyable. We were both angry. I do not think Donovan even ordered food. I placed my food in a to-go box. The day ended with Donovan being late for his next game. His assistant coach was coaching when we made it back to the gym. Donovan did not coach his team until the second half. I ended up leaving him at the gym for someone else to bring him home while I left, sobbing in the car as I drove home alone. This was one of many outbursts that I had. We would argue at church, at work (we both worked in the same place), at ball games, around our friends, around his family, and especially at home.

Even though I was having this deep inward and outward struggle with my marriage, I *really* loved the Lord, and I deeply desired to do the things He had called me to do. In the midst of all of the chaos of marriage, I began serving in the children's ministry at my church. It was and still is my personal conviction that I needed to be serving the body that I was and am a part of in some way, and although I did not really like kids, there was certainly a need for someone to serve the kids in the congregation that we were attending. Also, at this time, an opportunity arose to be a part of a minister's class. It was an opportunity for people who felt called to ministry to come together to learn how to write sermons, how to hear God's voice, and begin to prophesy. I already had some experience with prophecy, so this piqued my interest. I loved getting the opportunity to practice hearing God's voice, and I felt called to do ministry. Without hesitation, I signed my name on the paper and began attending the Sunday night ministry class.

As part of my journey to completing the very first LLTK, I reached out to the ladies I went to church with for help. I explained to them in the very beginning that I did not want this to be a church thing, but a Jesus thing. The itinerary was to have session one, complete with worship and our first speaker, followed by a catered lunch. We would finally end session two with our second speaker and closing worship. The ladies I consulted seemed to like the idea of being part of the conference and obliged to help. I had already done the legwork to book the speakers, the worship team, and even some of the prayer team. What I really needed help with was serving lunch and making sure there was enough food to feed the number of people who were planning to attend.

It was not until the second meeting I had scheduled for LLTK— the meeting in which we would assign the women who were interested in helping me execute this event to a specific team— that I discovered that asking a group of ladies to serve lunch at an event could be offensive. You see, the church that I now called home had an attendance of mostly African American people. While my husband had done an excellent job teaching me about his culture, we had never talked about the importance of phrasing conversations in a way that was well thought out and not offensive. When I asked a group of ladies to serve in the kitchen at our conference, they perceived *me* as wanting *them* to be "the help." Questions and comments started swirling around my husband, my mother-in-law, and our pastors. Questions like "Is she racist?" and "I think she just wants the Black people to be downstairs in the fellowship hall and the white people to be seen." I look back on that season now with grace and ambiguity. While I can see how my request could have been offensive, it was not the intent of my heart. In my perspective, the church had approximately six Caucasian people in it, including myself and the men. I was not asking ONLY the African American people to help with serving lunch; I was asking the ladies I went to church with if they could help. It just so happened that most of the ladies were African American. I had also never intended to leave any person out of the event, and it definitely was not in my heart to ensure that "only the white people were seen." In an attempt to create something culturally balanced, I asked my mother-in-law to share a word at the conference and had parties from multiple generations and races on the prayer team. Also, the serving of lunch was set up in such a way that no one had to miss any part of the conference. A few of the ladies who had volunteered to make sandwiches beforehand had arranged for their items to be dropped off either the night before the event or the morning of the event, and my mom, myself, and my best friend made several crockpots of taco soup, white chicken chili soup, and potato soup. All the volunteers would have needed to do was walk downstairs a few moments before the altar call following the end of the first session and put their gloves on.

I had not asked for volunteers to help set up before the conference, clean up after the conference, or do any of what most event organizers would call the "hard stuff." My best friend, mom, and I were planning to do all of that, but I would never get the chance to explain that. With a broken heart and a million questions about how the phrasing of one request could cause a group of people to believe that I was intentionally racially offensive, I decided it was best that I not cause any more friction. I canceled any further LLTK meetings; my mom, three ladies from my church whom I had a close relationship with, my husband, and my best friend rallied together to pull the event off.

I wish I could say that this was the extent of the church hurt that I suffered. Although I was sad about the events leading up to LLTK, I powered through, still attended church, and still attended my weekly Minister's Class meetings. It was not until one particular night at minister's class that the way I viewed "church" and the people who attended church (not this particular church, but church in general) would change forever. On this night, the leader of the class asked us to go around the room and tell each other what we thought were each other's hindrances to ministry. There were eight of us in the class, and, one by one, we went around the room and told each other what we *perceived* as each other's hindrances to ministry. Most of the comments people made to some of the others in the class were things like "You are too insecure," "You do not see your own value," and "You have too many kids to devote time to ministry." When it was time for the class to tell me my hindrances, I was told that I was rude, disrespectful, and arrogant. I did not know how to talk to people, and I was the reason that my husband's ministry would never be successful. Surprised at the words I was hearing, I was speechless. I recall sitting on my hands, just in total shock. I was completely still, but it seemed like the room was spinning out of focus. I was confused as to how people— people who loved Jesus—could say these things to someone. This did not feel like I was being told there were hindrances to my ministry; it felt like the people in the class had been armored up, lying in wait for this moment. The moment they could tell me all of my character flaws, the moment they could tell me what they really thought about me. While I was waiting for the class to end, I texted Donovan to come pick me up, as we only had one car. I had choked back tears for the majority of the class, but as soon as the door to my small, black Ford Fiesta shut, I sobbed. Tears warmed my red, puffy face for hours. Through sobs, I was able to explain to Donovan the events of the night, and although unsure what to say, he sat in silence with me and held my hand as I began to process.

In the days, weeks, and months after this particular night in ministry class, I started to fight the battle of depression. I often told people that I felt like I was in a small room. The room had no windows, no doors, and it was continuing to get smaller. I was suffocating in my own mentality and was unsure how to get free. My marriage was on the rocks, I was barely surviving the last semester of my senior year of college, we had absolutely no money, and in what I thought should have been my safe place, my church, I felt like hated me. I remember not wanting to live, but not wanting to die, either. Somehow, existing was not enough, but surviving took every ounce of strength I had. I was always miserable. I was either faking laughter or crying. I was always angry, and I was overall defeated. The life I dreamed of at thirteen, and the one I thought I was agreeing to when I said "I do" on an altar in front of all of my friends and family at twenty-two, had turned out to be a complete nightmare at twenty-three. The young girl, who felt like she had nothing to offer, had all of her insecurities about herself confirmed. She was heartbroken, unwanted, unaccepted, and unloved. At least, that's what she told herself every minute of the day. How would she survive?

Chapter

3

My husband's favorite place to sit and contemplate the meaning of life is the toilet. Nine times out of ten, you will find Donovan in the bathroom. For reasons that I cannot understand, that is his prayer closet. But, it is not only that. Donovan studies his Bible, reads books, journals, and even writes his songs mostly from the toilet seat. I recall one day at my lowest point, after a full day of arguing—okay, I do not know for sure that we were arguing that day; I just assume we were since we did most of the time—he called to me from the bathroom. I had been laying on the couch cuddling my sweet, orange tabby cat, Oliver. Most likely, I was scrolling on social media or texting my mom—perhaps both.

"Kayleigh, come in here," he said. I slowly drudged across my small apartment, making my way to the door of the room in which he was sitting. I cracked open the off-white door that had paint peeling off the bottom of it. "What do you want?" I grumbled. I always grumbled when Donovan would try to talk to me about my emotional well-being, and there was something in the way that he called my name that suggested he wanted to chat about my mental and emotional health. He said, "Come in here," and with hesitancy, I nudged the door fully open, and stepped into the bathroom just enough to close the door behind me.

Our apartment was very small—only about five hundred square feet. Our kitchen area was only about six feet long, and we had maybe five cabinets in total. Our oven was literally the size of a large air fryer. You could barely fit a frozen pizza in it, much less an actual pan to cook a real meal in; our stovetop had three burners, but it was also very small. You could only use two pans on it at a time because there was not enough room between the stovetop and the wall to place a pan that had a handle. I recall laying a cutting board across our small sink to give myself a little extra counter space when I needed to cut vegetables for our meals. Even though our kitchen was small, our bathroom, bedroom, and living area were a decent size. I was standing with my back against the bathroom door, still a little annoyed that Donovan called me in there. He said, "I want to talk." I had a glare in my eyes that told him I was curious about what he wanted to talk about, but I said nothing. I crawled on top of our bathroom countertop and sat crisscrossed. In an attempt to distract myself from the questions about my emotions that I knew were coming, I started to fidget with my pink, off-brand, cheap hair straightener and other items in my makeup case. It was obvious that I was using those items as a distraction; I had not cared about my hair being fixed or my makeup being done in months.

To my surprise, Donovan did not mention my mental or emotional health. He stated, "I feel like the Lord wants me to ask where you stand with Him." This question caught me off guard. I hated talking about how I was doing emotionally. I hated even more talking about how I was doing spiritually. Tears immediately filled my eyes and started to run down my cheeks. I answered Donovan's question truthfully, "I do not want anything to do with Him." I remember the tight, squeezing feeling I had in my chest as those words rolled off of my tongue. Donovan responded, "I think that is where you need to start to find healing." He was right, but how? Frustrated that the Lord would have Donovan ask me that question, I left the bathroom and went back to the couch to continue cuddling my cat and scrolling on social media. Distracting my mind was usually my best medicine, but it did not work in this scenario. My thoughts raced as I tried to mentally unpack how I actually felt about my relationship with the Lord.

That was not really true, was it? Did I really want nothing to do with God? I love the Lord, and I have spent twenty-two years serving him. Time would tell that I was not done with God, but as I began to process my own thoughts and evaluate how I ended up here—declaring that I did not want anything to do with God anymore—I realized that God was going to require me to change even if my circumstances never did. He was going to require me to forgive the people who had hurt me the most. He was going to force me to choose to love the man I wanted to leave. He was going to make me lay down my pride and my feelings that told me my bitterness, anger, and terrible attitude were justified. He was going to require that I give up too much control and comfort.

You may be wondering how I had control and comfort in the most heartbreaking season, but the reality was that I was well acquainted with my depression and bitterness. The depression gave me an excuse to be bitter and mean; bitterness and meanness kept people at bay. No one will argue with the prideful girl; she is never wrong. No one would confront the mean girl; her mouth is too smart. The bitter girl who refuses to forgive? People leave her alone, too, for fear of hurting her even more. My depression became a safety mechanism, up until Donovan posed his lovely question in the bathroom—a safety guard that I fully intended to carry forever. You see, it was easier for me to be depressed and guarded than to attempt to walk through the trauma of forgiving. Forgiving meant I would have to *actually feel* the emotions of pain and hurt fully and let God heal me from the inside out. The reality was that I did want God, but only in the ways that justified my sin. I wanted God to affirm my anger, depression, hatred, and bitterness toward the ones that hurt me. I stood on the scripture that tells us that vengeance belongs to the Lord while disregarding the other scriptures that command us to walk in love and to forgive. I wanted God to heal my heart and right every wrong without putting in any of my own personal effort to step toward healing. From my perspective, healing from the inside out sounded like a tumultuous process that I had zero interest in. What I knew then but did not care to try to acknowledge is that a holy God can love us while we deal with and struggle with sin. He cannot, however, justify our sin, no matter how justifiable it seems to be; He certainly cannot encourage us to stay sinful because it is convenient or comfortable for us.

"For the scripture says, 'You must be holy because I am holy.'"
1 PETER 1:16 (NLT)

The reality, not just for me but for all of us who are on our journeys to "become her," is that God will always require us to change. To grow. To be more like Him. What kind of God would He be if He did not push us or challenge us to be better? Jesus was the Holy Savior who laid down every ounce of pride so that He could die a painful, agonizing death. He was betrayed, mocked, and beaten, and they gave Him vinegar when He asked for water as He was hanging on the cross, gasping for air. They ripped the clothes off of His body and gambled for them. He foreknew all of this was going to happen, yet, when the Roman soldiers came to arrest Him as He stood in the Garden of Gethsemane, He looked at them and said, "Do what you came to do."

I cannot speak for you, but I am fairly certain that had someone come to me in my late teens and told me what my early twenties would look like had I chosen the path that I did, I would have backtracked and chosen the path of least resistance. But the path of least resistance would not have made me like Christ. Jesus, if you read through Matthew 26:53, essentially says He could have legions of angels rescue Him from what was to come. But He chose not to. He humbled Himself to the brutality of evil men, and He let God resurrect Him. Often, when we look at the very hard things we are facing, we have this deep desire to be rescued from them. I can recall weeping, begging God to rescue me from my marriage, from my church hurt, and from my depression. There are things in my life, even as I type this, that I wish to be rescued from. Yet, as I continue on my journey to "become her," I realize that my being rescued is not necessarily what is best for me. It is best that I lean into the brutality of whatever unfortunate circumstance lies before me and ask God for wisdom, guidance, and grace as I walk through it. My response to my circumstance should be like the one Christ had when Judas showed up in the Garden of Gethsemane.

"Do what you came here to do. I give you permission to mold me, shape me, change me, and make me more like the Father."

IDENTITY CRISIS

"Religion that is pure and undefiled before God the Father is this: to visit orphans, and widows in their affliction, and to keep oneself unstained by the world."
JAMES 1:27 (ESV)

I recall sitting in my car one night, crying, like I often did. I was praying, begging God to settle something in my marriage because I was certain that I would not make it out alive. I, at one point, remember having the exact thought that "I am going to have to kill him or kill myself because we cannot co-exist." I knew the shame of divorce was not something I wanted under my belt, and in the midst of an agonizing cry that must have touched the ears of Heaven, I finally heard the Lord say to me, "Be in the marriage, but not of it." I jotted down those words in my notes app on my iPhone like I often do. Even so, when I heard the Lord say things to me; I began to ponder what that meant. I knew it was a play on the popular phrasing I had heard in youth group all throughout my teens: *To be in the world but not of it.* This phrase was a reference to several scriptures in the Bible. Some in John (John 17:11, 14–15), Romans (Romans 12:2), and, of course, the scripture that is mentioned above, James 1:27.

To be unstained by the world...what did that mean? I am sure many people interpret this in many different ways, but to me, it means that the nastiness of the world does not define you, that Jesus defines you. So what if the world says you are no good, unwanted, not accepted, and messed up? Jesus says, come as you are. I want you; I accept you, and I love you. But how would this translate to my marriage? One thing I learned about myself as I started to allow God and His word to transform me was that my identity was out of place. I had this expectation that Donovan would complete me. *Our love would be unmatched.* We would be the couple that never fought, never went to bed mad, and would certainly never wake up still mad over last night's argument. We would do ministry together, have kids, be financially blessed, and our lives would be rainbows and butterflies. We, in fact, always fought, always went to bed mad, and never woke up thrilled about spending our days together. Life was the *opposite* of rainbows and butterflies; I was feeling unloved and unwanted. And then, when my church hurt occurred, it added another layer of frustration to my marriage. Not only did I feel like Donovan did not love or want me, but I felt like he was not a protector. When people had questions about whether or not I was racist, or comments about how rude and disrespectful I was, they brought them to him. I recall feeling like he offered people a safe place to complain about how much they disliked his wife, like it was his job to fix me. Oddly enough, I and the general public all had the same expectation for Donovan—for him to complete me or fix me. That expectation was not only out of order, but it was also out of the scope of his responsibility. After a few years, and a few hundred conversations, I know now that he never provided a safe place for people to talk about me. Every conversation that was brought to him regarding me was met with "You do not know her; you do not know what goes on in our home. Keep those thoughts and opinions to yourself." But in that season, there were not enough words in the English dictionary to convince me otherwise.

Unwanted. Unloved. Unaccepted. Unprotected. This was my self-acclaimed and accepted identity, and I was feeling all of those things as they related to my marriage. However, God showed me that I was feeling all of those things as they related to *Him*. Scripture talks about how we, the church, are the Bride of Christ and He is our bridegroom. I had only been married for a few months, but my physical husband had not met any of my expectations;

surely all bridegrooms were the same, right? My husband did not want me; why would God? My husband did not love me; why would God? My insecurities, emotions, and other people told me that I was not good enough for Donovan. Was I accepted or good enough for the King of Kings? Surely not. And would He protect me? Would He guard my heart, or would fully leaning into a relationship with God and letting **HIM** define me leave me with more unmet expectations?

I was unsure of the answer, but I did love Jesus, despite my words to Donovan when he posed the question regarding where I stood with God. It was as if my head knew that Jesus would love me, no matter what, that I was enough for Him, that He was a kind gentleman who would be careful with my heart. My head knew that Jesus accepted and wanted me. I just had to get my head to connect the dots to my heart and spirit; I had to learn how to be in this marriage without letting it identify me. Sure, I was Donovan's wife, but I was, and I am a daughter of Christ. I was not and am not made or defined by my marriage, or my husband, or anyone, for that matter. I was created by the King of Kings, knit together in my mother's womb, and made to complete every good work. I am smart. I am pretty. I am confident. I am wanted. I am accepted. And I am safe in the arms of the Father.

THE BEST ADVICE

"But when anything is exposed by the light, it becomes visible, for anything that becomes visible, is light..."
EPHESIANS 5:13 (ESV)

For the first few months of my depression, I suffered in silence. Eventually, though, as the Lord began to reveal things to me through His word, I started to invite people into my headspace who would speak life. Using scripture, God reminded me that light and dark cannot coexist. I knew the way to healing was to bring the dark things I was facing into the light. This was very challenging for me to do. At first, I felt incredibly stupid for struggling with depression. I mean, I was a Christian. We were supposed to have it all together, all the time, right? And even worse, at the root of my struggle with depression was a failing marriage and a conflict that I had run into at church. Surely, I was dramatic. I could hear people's eyes roll as I imagined talking about my struggle. "You were so spoiled growing up. How could you be *depressed?*" Your husband is so good at leading worship, and he loves people so well. What do you mean you are miserable? Get over it." Also, in the Christian world, sometimes there is this notion that because we have Jesus, we have to be okay all the time, and when we are not okay, we should just read our Bible a little more, spend a little more time in prayer, or worship a little harder.

Perhaps that would work for some people, but for me, I was **REALLY** struggling, and although I was saved, I did not feel as though I had Jesus. He felt far from me, out of reach. It was a struggle for me to get out of bed in the mornings. Reading my Bible felt like homework, and my prayers felt like they were falling on deaf ears. Also, the "do more" mindset that some Christians have regarding depression is dangerous. It suggests that those struggling with depression are not good enough Christians. I spent nearly two years depressed, and, in those two years, I did read my Bible, worship, and pray; I did all of the things you are "supposed to do" when you are struggling. While I would not advise anyone struggling with depression (or anything, really) to forsake doing those things on a regular basis, reading my Bible more, praying harder, and worshiping longer are not what brought healing into my life. Healing, for me, was a process that took months.

Nonetheless, despite seeing people's eyes roll as I *thought* about opening up to others about my struggles, I decided the risk was worth it. One of the very first people I spoke to about my struggle (aside from my spouse) was my mother-in-law. To most people, it probably seems a little unorthodox to speak to your mother-in-law about the struggles you are having with her son, but we had and still do have a good relationship. She was and still is a mental health professional, and she loves the Lord so much. If anyone could give me guidance on how to overcome this darkness, it would be her. I can recall the moment I decided to call her, like it happened yesterday. It had been raining off and on all day; the road was still damp with rainwater. Donovan and I had been chatting about my desire to be healed but my seeming inability to do so. Up until this point, no one knew that I was struggling with depression. I didn't even know. I mean, I *knew* I was sad all the time, and getting out of bed felt like a job. But I did not actually know I was depressed until I befriended WebMD. WebMD says that symptoms of depression include anxiety, excessive crying, loss of interest in once pleasurable activities, excess sleepiness, insomnia, weight gain, and repeatedly going over thoughts. It also lists several others, but these are the symptoms that I had.

After talking with Donovan about my self-diagnosed depression, he suggested that I call his mom. Knowing that I needed to talk to someone other than the man I desperately wanted to divorce, I called her. She answered, "Hello." With tears in my eyes and my voice shaking, I said, "I need to talk to you." She responded, "Are you okay? What is wrong?" I answered, "I think I am depressed." She asked, "What is going on that you would think that?" I proceeded to tell her all of the symptoms that I had of my self-diagnosed mental health disorder, and while I cannot recall if she affirmed my diagnosis, she did give me some of the best advice I have **ever** heard; it is advice I use even to this day.

She stated that she has struggled with depression before, and one of the best things she did was start going to therapy. At therapy, she stated, her therapist gave her the best advice she had received, and she would like to pass it on to me. The advice that was passed down to me was to "grieve every loss" and to "feel every emotion."

It was bizarre for me to think about feeling every emotion—the only one I had felt for some time now was sadness. I had forgotten that there were other emotions that existed. Still, I went on this journey of grieving every loss, but feeling every emotion came a little after my healing process had started. As part of grieving every loss, I made a list of all the losses I had suffered since being married. The loss of unmet expectations for what I thought marriage would be like. The loss of relationships and friendships I never got to have at the church I attended. I wrote down the mean things that had been said to me that I pretended did not cut at the time. The loss of not being financially stable. For what felt like hours, I scanned my heart and racked my brain to think of losses. And I wrote them down. After, one by one, I went through and prayed. I named them and said, "God, I grieve the loss of the expectations that went unmet in my marriage." And, although I could not feel the emotions at the time of the prayer, I essentially said, "I feel the emotions that come along with this loss, and I choose to heal from them."

I still make a practice of this in my life. Seasons change. Some seasons are marked by great joy, some with great loss, some with great pain and sadness, and others with immense pleasure. Throughout each season, I try to make a practice of grieving the losses and feeling the emotions that come along with each one. This practice prevents me from going back into a depression. You see, there are often things that trigger me, and sometimes I want to turn off my desire to thrive. Sometimes I feel it would be easier to be depressed than to put forth the continued intentionality to walk in healing, but nonetheless, depression is not my portion, and I refuse to go back to that—whatever it takes.

Chapter 4

MY FAVORITE STORY

One of my favorite characters in the Bible is Elijah. I could not put my finger on why, exactly. Maybe it is because he was prophetic, and as a prophetic person, I love to study the prophets of old. Perhaps I love him because he was so anointed that he could lay his body over the body of a dead child and see the child come back to life. Perhaps it was both of those reasons. But more than just those reasons, it was because he was relatable. One of my absolute favorite Bible stories is one that he is in the dead center of; it is one of my favorites because, as I read it, I am reminded so much of myself. Perhaps, as you read this chapter, you will be able to find yourself in this story, too.

The story begins in 1 Kings 17:1. Elijah prophecies that there will be no rain and no dew for some time. After he prophesies this, in versus two through six, God says to him to "depart from here and turn eastward and hide yourself by the brook Cherith, which is east from the Jordan. And the ravens brought him bread and meat in the morning, and bread and meat in the evening, and he drank from the brook." The very next verse says this: "And after a while, the brook dried up, because there was no rain in the land."

What is important in this part of the passage is that GOD TOLD Elijah to go into the wilderness, AND He was taking care of him there. Also, it is important to note that the brook was dry because of the prophecy Elijah had given—Elijah was at fault here for his own issue. I wonder how Elijah felt when the brook dried up. Was he annoyed with himself for the prophecy he had given? Was he annoyed with God? Did he ask God WHY the brook had to dry up in the place that HE told him to go, to begin with? Or was he comfortable being in the place of the dry brook because he knew that God would supernaturally provide for him there like He had been doing the whole time? If you continue to read through 1 Kings, you see that Elijah left the wilderness he was in because

God told him to go. Once he left, he encountered a widow who had planned to make one last meal for herself and her son. They would eat this meal and die, as they had no other food and no more money. Elijah asked her to give him their last meal, and then the Lord would bless her for her obedience. And bless her, did he! She never ran out of food again!

As I read this, I wondered how Elijah felt when God gave him the instruction to move out of the wilderness and into a different place. Elijah, although possibly annoyed with his water supply being cut off due to his own prophecy, was safe and comfortable in the wilderness, where God was sending him meals daily. This was a huge blessing, especially because during this period, Israel was in political turmoil. To leave the safety of the wilderness he was in could have been scary to him. It may have been easier for him to stay in the place where God was providing for him supernaturally versus moving into the next place God was calling him. Despite how he felt, he went out of the wilderness and into the next place God called him to. There, out of his obedience, he was able to be a blessing to a hungry widow and her child.

Moving through the story, after Elijah blessed the widow and her son, he presented himself to the King of Israel, Ahab. Ahab and his wife, Jezebel, were evil people. They were killers of prophets of the Lord, so Elijah presenting himself to the King was a huge deal. When Elijah presented himself to Ahab, Ahab said, "Is it you, you troubler of Israel?" Ahab, who was having to lead a nation through a drought—a nation that had no grass for their cattle to graze on, no water for their cattle or their people to drink, and no land that was producing crops—was most likely very frustrated with the prophet who prophesied this drought. I wondered to myself, as I was reading this, why he did not kill Elijah on the spot. He had killed so many other prophets, and this would have just been another one to add to his already high body count. Perhaps, it was Ahab's own motives at play; I suspect that he feared that if he killed the one who prophesied drought, the Lord would never bring rain.

Once Elijah confronted Ahab, he answered his question by essentially saying, "I have not troubled Israel, but you have because you have disobeyed God's commands, you've killed his prophets, and now you follow Baal." Baal was the Canaanite god responsible for rain. Elijah told Ahab to gather all of Israel to Mt. Carmel. And it was specifically said to gather the prophets of Baal, the ones who "sit at Jezabel's table." Once everyone was gathered at Mt. Carmel, Elijah asked the people of Israel, "How long will you falter between two opinions?" He continued, "If the Lord is God, follow Him, but if Baal, follow him." Elijah took two slaughtered bulls. He gave one bull to the prophets of Baal to prepare an offering, and he, a prophet of God, took the other for an offering. Elijah then informed the prophets of Baal along with all of the other Israelites who had gathered at Mt. Carmel what was going to happen. He explained both he and the prophets of Baal would pray to their gods, and the first people to have their offerings burnt up with fire from heaven were the ones who could say that their god is the Lord.

The prophets of Baal spent hours, praying and prophesying over their sacrifice. They cut themselves, making their body its own blood sacrifice, thinking perhaps that they would get their god's attention. After hours of the prophets of Baal praying, Elijah built his altar. He proceeded to fill four water pots, twice, and pour it into his altar. Each water pot could hold up to twenty-five gallons of water. This would mean that Elijah dumped two-hundred gallons of water on his offering. To say that his offering and the wood used to light the offering on fire was soaked would be an understatement. One thing that I find interesting in this part of the story that I wish to point out to you is that water, all throughout the Bible, has been something referred to that has the power to purify and bring deliverance. Also, water pots were mostly stone to prevent any impurities from entering the water after it had been placed in the water pots. Throughout the New Testament, water is related to referring to the Holy Spirit. Think of the women at the well in John, Chapter 4. She comes to the well because she is thirsty, but Jesus tells her He can give her water that will ensure she is never thirsty again. He is referencing the Holy Spirit. When Elijah poured water on the sacrifice, it was not just to drench it to show that God can burn up a completely drenched altar and sacrifice; it was a representation of the purity that was to come to an impure nation. Perhaps it was also to show the prophets of Baal at that time their need for purity in their sacrifice, but it also points us directly to Jesus and His ability to drench us in water that cleanses us and makes us like Him.

After Elijah drenched his sacrifice, he prayed that the Lord would send fire from heaven to burn up his offering. Fire fell from the sky and burned up every piece of drenched wood and soaking wet sacrifice. The full glory of God was certainly on display. After this, Elijah executed the prophets of Baal, just as Ahab executed the prophets of God. Next, Elijah told Ahab that he "hears an abundance of rain." Ahab was confused because it had not rained in years, and it was not raining when Elijah said those words to him. So what exactly did Elijah hear? He heard something in the spirit realm that would suggest that God is on the move naturally. Shortly after these words came out of the mouth of Elijah, rain fell. And not like a sprinkle of rain, a full-on downpour—an abundance. This brought redemption and life to the barren land. After the showdown on Mt. Carmel, the drought came to an end, and Ahab ran to Jezebel and told her all that had happened. Angry that Elijah slaughtered the prophets of Baal—her allies and friends, the ones who sat at her table—she threatened to kill Elijah by saying to him she "will have his head before the sun sets tomorrow." At that threat, Elijah retreated back to his safe place—the wilderness. There, he prayed for death.

Again in the wilderness, God sent angels who brought him food and drink. This food and drink must have had some anointing in it because it equipped him to travel forty days and nights to Mt. Sinai. When he arrived, he entered a cave and slept. There, the Lord spoke to him and asked him what he was doing. Elijah essentially said, "I have worshiped you, and prayed, and did everything right, and Jezebel has killed all of your prophets. I am the only one left, and she wants to kill me next." This was not an accurate statement. Certainly, other people in the world worshiped the true God, but it indeed showed how isolated Elijah felt and even how potentially disappointed he felt that God had allowed him to get to this point. God told Elijah to go stand outside the cave, and there the Lord passed by. As the Lord passed by, a windstorm strong enough to knock the rocks loose hit the mountain, followed by an earthquake, and a fire. But the Lord was not in any of these dramatic manifestations. After the fire, Elijah heard a still, small, quiet voice ask him again, "What are you doing here?" Elijah answered in the same way he did before by saying, "I have worshiped you, and prayed, and did everything right, and Jezebel has killed all of your prophets. I am the only one left, and she wants to kill me next." The Lord did not respond by validating his struggle or telling him to get out of his pity party. He gave him direction on how to move forward.

I am going to stop here with the story of Elijah, but you can read through the rest of 1 Kings, and through 2 Kings to learn about Elijah and his predecessor Elisha. You can see how Jezebel was killed, how the Lord saved and conquered Israel, and so much more. There is so much to learn and unpack in those two books. But for now, and for the sake of *this* book, I want to spend time unpacking and sharing how this story relates to me and my life.

HOW I RELATE

In 2016, when I stood on an altar in front of nearly three hundred people, saying wedding vows, I was fully confident that I was obeying God. I knew beyond a shadow of a doubt that this man I was marrying was handcrafted for me. There was and still is no person better suited for me than Donovan. When I followed my husband into the church that we chose to attend together and become members of, I was certain that I was following God. *I followed Him straight into the wilderness.* As believers, we associate the wilderness with a dry, arid land with little to no vegetation and dried-up rivers. But, actually, when you google wilderness and click images, lots of beautiful waterfalls show up, with green grass and berries to eat. I imagine this is what the "wilderness" looked like to Elijah immediately after the prophecy he gave; I suspect there was a quite lengthy lag between when Elijah prophesied no rain and when his brook dried up. I can see how, for a while, it appeared that the wilderness was safe, and, of course, it would be easy to follow God into that. I resonate with this. When I got married, my wilderness appeared to be full of like-minded Christ followers and a husband who would do anything for me. It was easy to follow God into a leafy, green rainforest. It was not until my brook dried up, I experienced church hurt, and started struggling with college, money, and depression that I realized that my expectations for marriage and for life were going unmet. At that time, I began to feel frustrated that my once lively, safe space was becoming arid and dry.

I pegged this question earlier in this book, and I wish to bring it up again because of its relevance to my story. The question was this: Was Elijah annoyed with himself for the prophecy he had given, and was Elijah annoyed with God as he began to realize the brook was running dry? Did Elijah ask God WHY the brook had to dry up in the place God called him, to begin with? As I began to realize my brook was drying up in my once bountiful, beautiful wilderness, my questions to God started to sound like "God, why did you tell me to marry this man?" And "Lord, why did you lead me to this church?" I was annoyed that God would lead me to a place that would eventually become dry and desolate, and I was equally annoyed at myself for agreeing to go there. How could I have been so naive to think that I was the exception to the rule—that things in life would come so easily to me, to us? I thought I would not have to fight for unity in my marriage. I thought that it would come naturally and easily because I loved the Lord. It never occurred to me that I should mentally prepare my mind for church hurt. That kind of hurt was something other people experienced, not me. Despite whatever frustrations I was feeling with God or myself, the reality is that the wilderness became my safe place. Just as God would supernaturally send birds with food for Elijah to the wilderness, God would also provide for us supernaturally as we were in our wilderness, too, with things like car ads in the mail.

The supernatural care God provided us with when we were debating on buying ramen or gas is not the only way I became content with being in the wilderness, though. I became content there in all facets. My mental health became a crutch. I would use it to skip church, skip out on marriage, and really, skip out on life by choosing to lay in bed 24/7. I had built up this hard, combative shell of a personality that would go to war with any person who tried to convince me to love my husband, forgive my fellow church members who broke my heart, or be more like Christ. I could even use my mental health as a crutch to be combative with Christ, which is where I found myself when Donovan asked me where I stood with God that night in the bathroom. I mean, honestly, who can argue with the constant excuse of depression? No one could invalidate my personal feelings. They could only disagree with how I was responding to them.

My mental health not only became a crutch for me; it became a part of me—my identity. I was no longer identifying myself as the daughter of the King; I was identifying myself as the depressed girl. The more I became comfortable with God supernaturally providing for me in the wilderness, the less willing I was to move out of that place to heal. It was true. I was deeply annoyed with God and myself that I was stuck in this wilderness, but staying there was going to be easier than healing. Healing meant that I would have to forgive people who did not deserve it. Healing meant that I would have to armor up and fight for my marriage. Healing meant that I would have to fight for my own spiritual and mental health. Certainly, I would have to follow Jesus out of the wilderness like He was directing me to, but what would await me on the other side? Would it be the Ahabs and Jezebels of the world? The ones who spewed so much hatred in the minister's class? Or would it be my purpose? I know one thing: I was not really interested in finding out. The wilderness and all the bitterness and unforgiveness my heart could hold would do me just fine. I was not thriving, but my walls were up and no one would hurt me again. And that was preferred.

Although preferred, it was not biblical. What I realize now, as I reflect on that season, is that, as believers, we often expect this cushy life. A life of financial overflow, a marriage of bliss, and that Jesus would always answer all of our prayers perfectly how we want Him to. I, too, expected that. But as a result of Adam and Eve's sin, suffering is now a part of the life we live; unfortunately, it is rarely a conversation in the body of Christ. Jesus suffered. He suffered when He, too, was led BY THE SPIRIT to the WILDERNESS to not eat, or drink, and be tempted by Satan himself for forty days and forty nights (Mark 1:12-15). Jesus suffered when He was in the Garden of Gethsemane, and He prayed that the cup of wrath that He was going to have to drink by going to the cross would pass Him by (Matthew 26:39). Jesus suffered as He was nailed to a cross (John 19:16–18). I am not at all suggesting that we should have the expectation that life should be hard, or that we should not be in pursuit of good things or things that bring us joy. I am simply pointing out that following Jesus does not exempt us from spending time in the wilderness where our hearts break and our brooks dry up. Sometimes we run out of money and patience. Sometimes marriage is hard, and parenting is difficult. Sometimes life is incredibly frustrating. But let me assure you, choosing to step outside of the wilderness—to start your journey of healing, loving harder, forgiving easier, and showing grace to the ones who do not deserve it—will be the absolute best thing you can choose to do. At least it was for me.

Chapter
5

EFFECTING THE NEXT GENERATION

I heard Alex Seeley do an altar call once for women who were struggling with infertility. She asked women who were struggling with infertility to raise their hands. I was watching the sermon on a live stream, but the cameraman angled the camera in a way that showed the hands of infertile women raising their hands all over the room. Alex said this. "Look around the room. Look around at the hands." She stated, "This is not a plan to steal the infertility of women; this is the plan of the enemy to rob the next generation of children who will be raised in God-fearing homes, and to rob the next generation of children who will carry the gospel to their generation." As she said that, I began to sob because I began to realize that many of the issues we face have little to do with us and more to do with our children. If I am depressed, church hurt, and struggling in my marriage, sure, **I AM** going to miss what God has for me, but I am not going to raise my children to be the God-loving and God-fearing children I dreamed they would become. **THEY** will miss **THEIR** purpose because I am caught up in my own wilderness. If we could grasp the concept that our decision to walk out of the wilderness we have barricaded ourselves into effects the next generation, I have a stark feeling we would sprint out of our own bitterness and insecurities and into the next place God is calling us to, regardless of what we fear awaits us on the other side. Elijah certainly did. If you recall from the last chapter, as soon as he left the wilderness, he greeted a woman and her son, who were planning to use their last bit of flour and oil to cook their last meal. They were going to die. Elijah's miracle that day that saved their lives would have never happened had Elijah chosen to stay in the safety of his wilderness.

I resonate with Elijah in some ways regarding this. I certainly did not perform any lifesaving miracles for a mom and her child. But about a year after coming out of the season of depression that

I was in, my husband and I opened our home through a kinship care agreement to two little boys. At the time, the oldest was one month shy of turning two, and the youngest was only seven months old. While the story of how these two came to live with us is too private for publicity in this season, it has the fingertips of God all over it, and my prayer is that one day I can share it in a way that brings fruit to readers. Those two little boys taught me everything I know about loving and leading toddlers. But I firmly believe that I would not have been able to welcome them into my home in a way that was good and godly had I not walked through letting God re-identify the misidentified parts of my heart, heal my crushed, church-hurt spirit, and show me how to walk in love and grace toward my husband, my church members, and even myself.

After Elijah performs a miracle, he presents himself to Ahab—the enemy. The enemy says, "Is that you, you troubler of Israel?" This part makes my spirit leap with joy because it is how I feel like I was greeted by Satan when I left the pit of my depression and began to heal. I imagine myself in this cinematic moment, where I am dressed like Katniss Everdeen from the movie *Mockingjay*. I have been pushed down this muddy pit, and the enemy is standing on top of the ravine shouting, "I did it! I crippled her with depression; she's not coming back from this!" And as he is shouting, I'm climbing my way back to the top of the ravine. Dramatic music plays as I finally get to the top. I am muddy, bloody, and tired, and he looks at me with a grimacing glare and says, "Is that you, oh troubler of Madisonville?" The reality is that I am not a troubler of my city, nor was Elijah the troubler of his. Ahab—the enemy—was the troubler, and I am a troubler to the schemes of the enemy that seek to destroy my home, my city, my state, and my nation. You are also a troubler to the plans of the enemy. So climb out of your pit in your Katniss Everdeen costume and say. "I am no troubler of my town. You are the troubler. And you thought you had me, but I will trouble your plans to bring destruction to my life, and my family. Because, regardless of how you have tried to label me as the depressed girl, or the abused girl, or the broken girl, I now identify as the healed girl. And I have the battle scars to prove it."

Next, God tells Elijah to gather up the prophets of Baal, namely the ones who sit at Jezebel's table. When I was struggling with depression, I came to a place where I was asked to name and grieve my losses. I did not realize it until writing this, but I was being asked to round up the things in my life that are seated with the enemy and bring them before the Lord. The bitterness, the unforgiveness, the unmet expectations, the depression—all of it. Not so it could be on display, but so it could be burnt up and done away with, and so that my heart could be purified in the process with pure water that only comes from the Holy Spirit. Even as I type these words on this page, I sense God asking the same thing of you. What things in your life need to be brought before the Lord so He can deal with them accordingly? What emotions, thoughts, and struggles are you facing that are seated with the enemy? The next question that is presented in this story is this: "How long will you falter between two opinions? If the Lord is God, follow Him, but if the Lord is Baal, follow him."

That night in the bathroom with my sweet husband, the night that he said, "I feel like God wants to know where you stand with Him," that was the equivalent of Elijah asking the people how long they would falter between two opinions. Through the mouth of Donovan, God was saying, "Kayleigh, how long will you falter between wanting to be healed and wanting to be comfortable in your misery?" After Elijah asks this question, God sends fire from Heaven to burn up the offerings—both of them—the offerings from Elijah and from the prophets of Baal. Once the prophets of Baal are done away with, God sends an abundance of rain. Notice how the dryness of the wilderness was not quenched until the glory of God was put on display. That seems to be how it is in our own lives. It is almost never until we stop faltering between two opinions and we choose God and His purposes for our lives that He sends the good stuff—the fire to burn up the things that do not belong, and the moisture that our dry, weary souls are so desperately craving.

LET'S BACKTRACK

I have told you one of my favorite Bible stories, how I relate to it, and I have even shared some revelations about what God has shown me regarding where you may find yourself in this story. What I have not shared is what healing actually looked like for me. Elijah walked right out of the wilderness, started doing miracles, and saw the glory of God manifest in this great showdown during the battle of the prophets on Mt. Carmel. This was not my story. Healing was a process that took several years for me, and sometimes it is still a battle. While I am no longer depressed, I do still have big emotions that I struggle to process. Although it has been years since I sat in the parking lot of the county clerk's office debating on walking through the doors and filing for divorce, I am certain that marriage is not for the weak. I am a firm believer that a little time, a lot of Jesus, a few friends in your corner who can shoot you straight, and the ability to have grace for yourself and for others can heal all wounds—that is how I healed. But even that sounds easier than it was, so let me break it down for you.

HEALING BEGAN

It was February 3rd, 2018. My eyes were open long before my alarm went off. My best friend, a lady from our church, and myself had spent months planning and preparing for this day. It was the day of our second Love Like the King Women's Conference, and we had a mile-long list of things to accomplish before 8 a.m. I had woken with a sense of dread, not because I hated LLTK or did not want to go, but because I hated life. Just the thought of hosting an event was enough to kick my depression into overdrive. I was physically exhausted before my feet touched the floor.

Despite my feelings, tasks still had to be accomplished. I delayed my responsibilities the morning of the conference by taking a nice, long, hot shower. My hair was short at the time, and I did not wear much makeup, so drying and straightening my hair took no time at all; I could also put on a full face of makeup within seven minutes. I already knew what I was going to wear. We had solid gray tee shirts made that said "Love Knows No Limits" on them as a fundraiser for the conference. I paired my new shirt with a cardigan in a darker gray, and I was out the door.

Before making my way to the church, I needed to go grab donuts and orange juice for the volunteers, run by the ATM, and go to my mother's house and grab the chalkboards to finish decorating the foyer before people started to arrive. The worship team had already arrived; they were setting everything up for the sound check. The men in the church were recruited to serve the women lunch. Many of them were there also, anticipating the arrival of donuts. Upon my arrival, one of my and Donavan's friends, Dustin, greeted me with a friendly "Hello." He was one of the worship leaders, and he stated that he was "so excited for what God is going to do today" and that he "had been praying over this day for weeks." I responded by saying, "Well, I am glad someone has because I absolutely do not want to be here." He appeared shocked at my honesty, and truly, sometimes my honesty shocked me, too. He asked what I would rather be doing. I responded, "Lying in bed." I do not recall how the rest of that conversation went, but eventually, we went our separate ways. Even though my depression nagged me to stay in bed all day, there was a conference happening, and we both had things to prepare.

The morning of the conference went smoothly. During the worship set for the first session, I ran between the sanctuary and fellowship hall, ensuring that there were no issues getting lunch set up for the ladies. After worship, I settled into a seat on the very back row next to my mom and listened to the speaker. It is rare, even now, that I take the time to listen to a speaker that was invited to LLTK. Usually, I find myself at the registration table or fixing the projector. But this day was different. I had never heard this particular person share their testimony, and I wanted to.

The speaker shared about how she grew up, and how she had a child outside of marriage when she was very young. She spoke about how she did not want to have any more kids without a husband, so when she got pregnant a second time, she found herself at an abortion clinic. She talked about how, as a result of her abortion, she struggled with her mental health. She was depressed, and her heart was full of shame. She spoke about how God redeemed her from all of that and told of how she is flourishing in her walk with God now. *Flourish...I had not flourished in months.* After her talk, the worship team came forward. They were playing the melody of *Break Every Chain* while the speaker was giving her altar call. She stated, "I believe that God wants to heal people from depression and free them from shame this morning. If you are dealing with any of those things, I want you to come forward, and someone will pray for you." At this time, I was still sitting in the very back row next to my mom, and God began to nudge my heart. Silently, for several minutes, God and I had an argument that only I could hear. "Go to the front, Kayleigh," He said. "No," I replied. "Kayleigh, go." "I will not." "Kayleigh, you need this. I will meet you there." My pride responded. "I will not go to that altar and ugly cry in front of people that I invited here. I am not going."

One by one, several people walked to the altar and received prayer. It seemed like God was meeting everyone there, just as He promised He would me. With great hesitancy, I walked to the front, my thoughts racing. *Only a handful of people know that I am depressed, now everyone is going to know. What are these people going to think of me? God, you better meet me here. I am halfway up there with everyone in the room looking at me. Gosh, I am already crying.* Once I got to the front, one of my favorite people on the Earth, my greatest mentor, and spiritual mama, met me on the altar. She grabbed me and began to pray. By this time, the worship team, still playing *Break Every Chain*, had settled in on one song lyric. The words "*I hear the chains falling*" echoed through the sanctuary while I was receiving prayer. I am not sure what Sister Marsha's prayer was, or what she prophesied to me, but my knees quivered as I fell to the ground. and I began to violently sob. I sat on the floor for what felt like an eternity; as tears rolled down my face, chains of depression broke off my heart. God certainly met me at the altar that day, and I have not been the same since.

THE HARD STUFF

Although the symptoms of depression were gone in an instant— the desire to sleep all the time, crying at the drop of a hat, the lack of interest I had in church, working out, and other things— healing was not instant. There was still some hurt, bitterness, and unforgiveness in my heart that I had to work through. When God broke the depression off my heart, He ripped off the bandages that I had used to cover up my heart wounds. I had to re-feel my hurt. I had to let God settle it. This took time and intentionality. After months of not reading the Bible or spending time in worship, I began to do those things regularly. Also, due to my depression, I had slipped into this pattern of not wanting to do anything—not the dishes, not the laundry, not going to the gym—absolutely nothing. When God began to heal my depression, I made sure that anything I thought about not wanting to do, I did anyway. I never wanted to do the dishes, and I still do not. That is my least favorite chore, along with folding laundry. But for months,

I made it a point to do both of those things regularly. Working out? I hated it. And, for several months, I intentionally went to the gym because I understood that doing things I did not want to do was going to force me to heal.

Also, as part of my healing process, I knew that I needed to forgive. As part of my journey to grieving every loss and feeling every emotion, I began to write letters to the people who I felt hurt me the most. These letters explained what I felt my accuser did to cause hurt, the specific emotions their words and actions made me feel, and they informed the people that they were forgiven. To the ladies who told me I was the reason my husband's ministry would never be successful, I wrote a letter. I wrote letters to Donovan and to those who accused me of racism, and although I did not share the letters with every person, it was freeing to name my accuser and write I forgive you on paper. It took time, but anger was replaced by forgiveness, and bitterness was replaced by grace. Perhaps the hardest part of healing, forgiving, and growing in my marriage in the days, months, and even years after those initial chains of depression were broken off of me was realizing my own sin. I had to come to terms with the fact that, although hurtful, those harsh words spoken to me at that minister's class that night were not one hundred percent wrong. I was living my life without regard to other people's emotions— rude. Although I do not feel as if I was arrogant, if people actually believed I was racist, I could see why they would use the term arrogance to define me. I was definitely outwardly disrespectful to Donovan—people took notice. And, had I continued to be disrespectful to him, and had we continued to live life selfishly, never developing a form of unity in our marriage, his music ministry probably would have been unsuccessful.

I do not say any of this to invalidate the hurt these words caused. I share this only to annotate how I grew from the hurt. It took several years to get to the point of self-reflection; do not compare my story to yours. Although I wrote this to share things God showed me, we are all on our own timelines of healing. What took me four years could take you months, and what took me three years may take you seven. We are all on our own journey to "become her," so please remember that as you read this chapter and continue to read the rest of the book.

Chapter

6

THE PROMISE OF RESTORATION

While Donovan enjoys sitting on the toilet for relaxation, I prefer a hot, steamy bath. You know, the kind where your whole body is the shade of a garden tomato when you get out of the tub and begin to dry off. One evening, sitting in my bathtub, I began to cry out to Heaven. Our bathroom, as I stated previously, was a decent size, and we did not have a shower curtain on our tub. We had those frosted glass sliding doors that were beautiful, but also a headache to clean. When the doors to the shower were closed, you obviously could not see anything that was behind them—that is how they were designed, for privacy. But no amount of frosted glass doors could hide my emotional exposure before Heaven on this particular night. My depression was gone, but my marriage was still struggling. My heart was still hurting, as I had not yet completely forgiven all of those who had caused me hurt. I needed to know that the journey that I was on was going to be worth it. I needed to know that my marriage was going to be one that would bless people. I needed to know that the tears I was crying on my way to church every single Sunday morning as I begged Donovan to let me stay home because I did not want to be around people whom I felt hated me were not in vain. I needed to hear God. I had felt Him at LLTK break the depression off me. But I needed to hear His voice. And finally, clear as day, the Lord said, "Be patient. I will bring unity to your marriage, and I will restore your honor in your church."

I am not sure what I wanted God to tell me that night as I was crying out to Him in my bathtub, but "Be patient, and let Me work" was not it. So, although I felt a little relieved that God had spoken to my frustrated, still bitter heart, I was still not sure what those words meant. I was fresh into the second year of my marriage. How long was I going to have to wait for some form of unity? And what did it mean for God to restore my honor? Over time, I learned how to not just survive my marriage. Donovan and I would begin to do better than we ever had, and I would soon find out just how God would restore my honor.

A GOOD LEADER – A GOOD HUSBAND

One of my favorite stories in the Bible is one that tells of Joshua and Caleb. They were excellent leaders, and because, biblically, a husband is the leader of the home, he could learn a lot from them.

Starting in Numbers 13, Moses commands twelve spies to go into the Promised Land and spy on it. Among those twelve were these two, Joshua and Caleb. Joshua and Caleb were two very young, faith-filled boys. They had previously been enslaved by Pharoah. They were rescued by Moses, experienced the Red Sea being parted, drank water from a rock, and ate manna that literally rained down from Heaven; if God could part seas, make water spray from a rock, and rain manna from Heaven, certainly, they believed He could do anything. After they had spent forty days spying out the land—the land that God was leading the Israelites to—they came back to give a report. The report was that the land was beautiful—truly flowing with milk and honey. Flowing with milk meant that there was plenty of pasture for cattle to graze in, and honey suggested there was plenty of farmland. Unlike the arid wilderness the Israelites had just journeyed through as they left Egypt, this new land was fertile, full of many different types of fruit. It was, however, not going to come without a cost. God was willing to give the land to the Israelites, but the groups of people who already occupied the land were not as willing to let the Israelites in. Not only were those who lived in the land unwilling to share, but they were also very large people. In Numbers 13:3, Caleb describes him and the other eleven spies as the size of grasshoppers compared to them. The people in the land were giants. The Israelites would have to **war against giants** in order to take the land.

In true Israelite fashion, the group began to groan and weep. They questioned why God would bring them into the wilderness to let them die, and even suggested killing Moses and naming a new leader to take them back to slavery. Despite Joshua and Caleb's efforts to convince them that God was on their side—that they could win any battle against any group of people because they had favor—the Israelites decided they would not enter the Promised Land. Joshua and Caleb were at a crossroads. They could leave the group, and go into the land God had promised them, they definitely had the faith to slay the giants in the land. I believe without any doubt that had they chosen to go into the land without Moses and the rest of the Israelites, they could have thrived in the land flowing with milk and honey. The other option Joshua and Caleb had was to stay in the wilderness with a faithless generation who was not physically, spiritually, or emotionally ready to step into the fertility of their promise. The greatest leaders, perhaps, in all of the Old Testament chose to forgo **THEIR** promise from God and follow a faithless generation back into the wilderness—praying and hoping that one day they would reach their destiny.

Donovan reminds me very much of Joshua and Caleb. As I reflect on those early years of marriage, I remind myself of a faithless generation. When Donovan and I got married, we had these big dreams. We both felt called to full-time ministry. I felt a calling to preach, and Donovan felt called to do music. We knew we loved Jesus, we loved our community, and we just wanted to make a difference in our area and leave a legacy behind. We were certain that God was leading us to a Promised Land of our own and that the day of "I do" was just solidifying that. But, when I encountered the giants—the church hurt, the misery of marriage, the struggle with money—I turned into an Israelite. My attitude became that of those who were asking God to "lead me back to slavery." Only, my cry was "God lead me back to my mama's house." But Donovan was truly the Joshua and Caleb of our marriage. He was sent out to spy on the fertility of our dreams—the promise of ministry.

A good leader always recognizes where their followers are, and just as Joshua and Caleb realized their followers were not ready for the Promised Land, so did Donovan realize that with me. I am so sure that he could have signed the dotted line on the divorce documents, and taken his Promised Land alone, leaving me in the wilderness to fend for myself. But he did not. Donovan took it upon himself to create a space for me to heal in. He knew that I was not going to heal at the church we had been attending due to all of the hurt that had occurred there. When a worship leader position became available at the church where my uncle (the one who married us) pastors, Donovan accepted it. For a season of time, Donovan pressed the pause button on releasing music and booking events for Don Ready Music, and—the icing on the cake— the week that Donovan accepted the worship leader position at the church my uncle was pastoring at, a house came up for rent that was pet friendly, within our budget, and just happened to be next door to my parent's house—my childhood home. At this time, God began to do something in my heart toward my husband. I started to realize that he loved me. Not like the "buy you flowers and send you an 'I love you' text in the middle of the day" kind of love. No, this was the kind of love that forewent his Promised Land to willingly go back into the wilderness with a faithless wife who was still hurting.

I do not believe that Donovan necessarily wanted to leave the church we were at to go and lead worship at my uncle's church. But he recognized that going to a place where I was certain that the leadership loved me, and the members did not have a tainted view of me due to a lack of communication or a miscommunication was going to be so instrumental in my healing, processing, and forgiving journey. He was right. Also, Donovan choosing not to release any music or book many events for Don Ready for a while was very healing to my heart. While there were some other reasons he did not release music other than just me, like us getting full guardianship of two of the most perfect little boys my heart has ever encountered, his choice to take a break from releasing music settled something in my soul. Scripture talks about how a man should love his wife like Christ loved the church, and it discusses how a leader in the home should present his wife as holy. For the first time since getting married, I realized that Donovan did actually love me like Jesus did; that he was willing to lead me in a direction of holiness and was also willing to give up every ambition and dream he had to ensure his wife was healed and our marriage was thriving.

Besides moving to a new church, and pressing pause on music, we also moved into a new home. This home was the absolute sweetest blessing, and it was the icing on the cake for me as I walked through a healing and forgiving journey. This house provided us with the opportunity to take care of two little boys who needed us. There is no way four people and three cats could have lived in a one-bedroom apartment. This house also provided me with the opportunity to live next to my mom. I mentioned way earlier in Chapter 2 that my mom was my best friend, and due to our car situation and how busy our schedules were, she and I were not getting to spend much time together. All of that changed when I moved next door to her, and man, oh man, has it been healing to my soul to be close to her? I distinctly remember waking up one morning very ill. It was around 5:30 a.m., and I was lying in my bed, crying quietly, so as not to wake my snoring husband. Every muscle in my stomach ached from vomiting, and my throat was so incredibly sore. I knew my mom would be awake because she worked from home and got started very early. I knew she would comfort and take care of me, and I knew I could rest there. Without hesitation, I walked across the yard, curled up in my childhood bed, and slept soundly for hours. This may sound silly to some, but after two (or more) years of fighting depression, struggling in my marriage, and sobbing on my way to Sunday morning church, there was something so safe and secure about this new season. I was able to spend time in my childhood home with my parents; I was attending a church in which my uncle was the pastor; and for the first time since being married, my husband's music career was not at the forefront of his mind—it was the healing of our marriage. Certainly, I was in a place of comfort and security, perhaps for the first time in nearly three years.

I truly believe that had life stayed absolutely the same for me— we never changed churches, changed where we lived, or even changed anything in the rhythm of our marriage—I would have found a way to survive. I may have found healing; I may have found a way to thrive in my own independent way. But I do not believe that we would be as blessed as we are now. God certainly honored Donovan for all of the sacrifices he made in that season, and now, here we are, nearly four years later. Donovan has nearly 225,000 followers on Instagram, and he has over 500,000 monthly listeners on Spotify. At this point, he has gotten to open for many more people, many people including David Crowder, KB, and Big Daddy Weave. He was recently invited to Lecrae's studio in Atlanta and has been getting more booking requests than he could imagine. Donovan is still the worship leader at the church he agreed to lead worship at in 2019, and now I do kids church and nursery with my cousin and aunt. I visit my mom very often, as we still live next door. We run errands together almost every weekend when Donovan and I are not out of town for an event, and we walk our dogs together almost every night in the summer. I hesitate to say that we are in the Promised Land yet. There are still things that we trust and believe in God for, but we are certainly not in the wilderness, and I attribute that, first, to Jesus, and second, to Donovan's Joshua and Caleb-like leadership.

RESTORATION OF HONOR

I wrote earlier about how the Lord told me that He would restore my honor. In the year 2020, just two weeks before the world got locked down for COVID-19, we had our annual Love Like the King Women's Event. It was a blast, truly my favorite conference to date, and we have had seven. My goal at every conference that we put together is to create a multi-generation, multicultural conference. I never want anyone to leave feeling like the event my team and I put together was not culturally or generationally balanced. In an effort to create that balance, that year we brought in DeeDee Freeman. She was a very popular minister in the late 80s and early 90s and a favorite among middle-aged African American women. She brought that multicultural, multi-generational feel to our conference, and we loved having her.

Because of who she was, and the type of crowd she drew, a lot of people from the church that I previously attended were present; a few of the people in attendance were those who had said those cruel words to me in our minister's meeting all of those years before. Along with DeeDee Freeman, we also had a lady there named Carla Pratico; she was a gem and amazing to work with. Carla is a lady in leadership in her hometown of New York City, and she is all too familiar with the amount of money it takes to organize and execute women's events. At the very end of the conference, before dismissal, Donovan stepped onto the stage to take up an offering. Before he could, Carla asked if she could have the microphone, stating that she would love to take the offering up. At this point, Carla, Donovan, and I were the only people standing on stage, and she asked me to take off my shoes and place them in front of the stage. I was hesitant to take off my shoes because, like always, I had on mismatched socks. I took them off, and she placed my shoes at the very front of the stage. Carla then said, "If this conference was worth anything to you, and you want to contribute to what Kayleigh and her husband are doing, I want you to bring your offering forward and place your money in her shoes. Because these shoes carry the Gospel."

As people began to bring forward their money and place it in my shoes, I stood on the edge of the stage, sobbing. Row by row, people walked up and placed hundreds of dollars in my stained Nike forces. All of this took place in front of the same people who told me I was rude, arrogant, disrespectful, and the reason my husband's ministry would never be successful. I felt like I was publicly honored by a person who, other than a few conversations, had no idea who I was, but more than that, for the very first time since 2016–2017, I felt honored by God. And I felt like He kept his word to me—the same word He spoke to me in the bathtub that night regarding my honor and my marriage. I usually leave every LLTK completely wrecked—in awe of God and His goodness. While it is true that I put LLTK together to be a blessing to our community, God blesses me at every single conference. But this conference was different. My friend Maegan and I took Carla back to her hotel in Nashville, and I sobbed the entire way there, relishing in the goodness of God and just weeping over how much He blessed me at that particular conference.

BACK TO ELIJAH

I shared the story of Elijah earlier. I also told you about the showdown on Mt. Carmel, where God proved himself mighty and strong. The very next thing that happens is Elijah saying, "I hear an abundance of rain." A few moments later, rain clouds begin to gather in the sky, and out of those clouds comes a torrential downpour that brings water to a dry, arid land. Surely, this season of healing—the season of church changing, house moving, kids getting, and music stopping—this was the season that proved to be my "abundance of rain" season. This was a season that brought peace and healing to my dry, weary soul. I was finally out of the wilderness, and my brook was flowing with water.

Chapter
7

Right after God used Elijah to move in the mightiest way, Jezebel said, "I will kill you before the sun sets tomorrow." And with no hesitations, no questions asked, and no doubt about the word of the enemy being true, he retreated back to his safe space—the wilderness—and there he prayed for death. The Lord gave him food and drink and sent him on a long forty-day journey. At the end of the journey, Elijah found rest in the cleft of the rock—the same cleft of the rock where it is believed God instructed Moses to go while he waited for the glory of God to pass him by in Exodus 33:22. The cleft was safe, and the cleft seems to be where, throughout scripture, God shows up.

CREVASSE

Have you ever seen the TV show called *I Shouldn't Be Alive*? If you have, you know that in this show, adrenaline seekers go out and do very dangerous things to find a "thrill. Oftentimes, these thrill seekers find themselves on death's doorstep, begging and pleading for help. It is usually by a mere miracle that these thrill seekers make it out of their journeys alive. In this particular episode of this show, these avid climbers climbed up Mount Rainier. They made it to the top, and they relished the beautiful view that the top of the mountain provided them. After a while, they began their descent back down the mountain. On their way down, their gear deceived them, and they misstepped. This caused them to fall into a deep crevasse. While in the crevasse, one mountain climber passed away while the other watched. The surviving mountain climber screamed for help for hours before realizing that no one from the surface of the mountaintop could hear him screaming for help from eighty feet below the surface. The surviving victim had two options. He could sit with his friend's deceased body in the crevasse and wait for the freezing temperatures to kill him, too, or he could try climbing eighty feet to the top of the crevasse. As this man began his journey to the top of the crevasse, he faced full-body exhaustion from climbing, malfunctioning gear, and melting ice chunks. These ice chunks were not normal size—some of these chunks were the size of refrigerators. If any one of these exceptionally large, very heavy ice chunks were to hit him as he was climbing, he could have been sent plummeting to the bottom of the crevasse again. Once the survivor was at the top of the crevasse, he was able to flag down help from a park ranger and get rescued. They were also able to recover the deceased victim's body and his family was able to have closure.

There is a stark difference between a cleft in a rock, which is something typically used for protection, and a crevasse. A crevasse is—according to the story above—something that is typically very deep and not really a safe place found in the rock. It is quite the opposite, actually. However, as God began to move me into a cleft of the rock, I did not associate it with a place of protection or safety. I identified it more as a place of obscurity, a place where I was isolated, where no one heard my bitter weeping. I felt like I was crying out for help, yet I was so far buried underground that help was not coming. No, this was not a place of God's protection. This was a place, a season, where it felt like every single person, place, and thing in it was meant to harm me. I was convinced that I was the only one for me. I was going to have to save myself. But how did I get to this point?

COVID-19

The year 2020 kicked off to be one of the greatest yet. We had moved into our new house, and our marriage was doing better than it ever had. I just started a new job, and our finances were looking better than they ever had. The two boys that I love so deeply had been living with us for seven months, and although I was not their biological mom, being a mom to them was my favorite part of life. In February of 2020, we paid Dr. DeeDee Freeman to come and preach at our women's event, LLTK 2020, and this was our most successful conference yet. We had almost four hundred women there, which is huge for something in our very small, rural area. So many testimonies came from LLTK that year—stories of how God laid it on some hearts of the women to start ministries; women were set free from depression, anxiety, anger, and even addictions. The way that God was moving upon the ladies in attendance was certainly a sight to behold. If there had ever been a season full of abundant rain in my life, this was it. Just as the two mountain climbers in the story I told above were beholding the beautiful sights that the top of Mount Rainier allowed them to witness, so was I beholding the beauty in my own life. I could have stayed in that season of abundance forever.

Two weeks later, with no warning and no time to prepare, the world shut down. "Two weeks to stop the spread" turned into almost two years at home, and whether willingly or by default, we were all forced into a safe place—a place away from the coronavirus. I was sent home from my job with mere minutes to pack up all of my equipment and get out of the office. I recall walking back into my office almost eighteen months later; it was like a time capsule; my ink pen was still in the exact same spot I had left it; my calendar was still flipped to March 2020; and my papers from my appointments I had the day I left were still on top of my shred pile. It was very surreal, almost creepy. The boys were sent home from daycare with no estimated date on which they could return. For months, we were unable to attend church or go to restaurants. The normal became cooking every meal at home, watching church on a live stream, working from home, and home-schooling kids. The only time we were not at home was when we were out driving around with our own family just to get out of the house or taking a walk or bike ride through the neighborhood. There really was nothing else to do.

Eventually, time moved on. Restaurants opened back up for business, churches opened back up for service, and schools and daycares opened back up along with other places of employment. It seemed like time had moved on for most people, but that was not the case for me. If you have made it this far, you know that I am a huge Taylor Swift fan, and there is this song lyric that she sings on an album she released during the pandemic. It says this: "Did you hear about the girl who got frozen, time went on for everyone else, she won't know it. She's still twenty-three, inside her fantasy, how it was supposed to be."

Shortly after the pandemic began, in April, to be exact, the two little boys that I had spent the last ten months loving were taken out of my home with no warning. I had only a few hours to pack their things and say goodbye. Because this was a family agreement, not something that was necessarily handled through the courts, AND we were in the middle of a pandemic, there was no way to fight this. I had to let them go. I could write an entire book on that situation itself—how it felt unfair and unjust and why it felt that way—but that is something to be shared when I fully understand why God allowed things to unfold the way they did. While I do rejoice in the reunification of families, and it brings me great joy to see the way the boys and their mom love each other, at first, losing them felt like losing my own kids, especially after ten months of raising them. The day we brought them into our home, we were under the impression that we would be adopting them. It never occurred to me that I would find myself sobbing over the toys that got left in their playroom and the pizza rolls that got left on the kitchen table. It certainly never occurred to me that I would still find myself crying almost three years later. Two weeks after losing the boys, one of my cats died, and around that same time, Donovan and I had close friends in our lives who seemed to be stepping out of the picture. We were just in a season of loss in our personal lives, on top of being forced to live in utter seclusion from those we worked with, attended church with, and our closest friends and family.

To say that my heart was completely shattered for the majority of 2020 would be a gross understatement.

This once beautiful mountain that I was standing on top of started to feel like something that was going to take me out. Soon after we entered this season of loss, I began to move into this place of doubting every single thing I knew about myself and the giftings and talents God gave me. If getting the boys was a God thing, but now they are no longer here, surely I did not know the voice of God. Was I even prophetic? Was I called to do LLTK? Was I supposed to marry Donovan? What else had I thought God had opened a door for that I walked through that I was unknowingly possibly disobedient in? My mental health was spiraling. I was in that place where Elijah found himself—back in the wilderness. However, I was not praying for death to overtake me. This is where Elijah and I differed. I had been depressed before, and I did not like that version of myself. I began to pray that God would rescue me from racing thoughts before those thoughts turned into a full-on depression. I needed a safe space for my mind to rest, I needed to hear God speak. I am still so thankful that the answer to my prayer came quickly.

Just a couple of days after these thoughts began to take my mind into captivity, this lady who had attended LLTK in 2020 posted a video online and tagged me. In the video, she stated that she was at the most recent Love Like the King Women's Conference. She stated that during an altar call, God healed her from being angry at HIM over the loss of her dad. She stated that her dad passed many years ago, and she spent every single one of those years angry at God for taking him away. She thanked me then and has thanked me several times since then for my obedience to do LLTK because there, God set her free. As I watched that video, I sobbed; I repented for doubting His voice in my life. As I write this and reflect on that season, I would identify this moment as the moment that God placed me in the cleft of the rock. In those early days of deep grief that my heart suffered as we lost kids, pets, and friends, I needed God to intervene, and He certainly came quickly with encouragement. What I did not realize, however, was that as I sat in the cleft of the rock, crying out to Jesus for healing for my sad heart, more trials would come that would seek to get me out of the cleft quicker than I expected. My cleft was feeling like a crevasse, and I was feeling like I was going to have to rescue myself.

CREVASSE OR CLEFT

Continuing through the story of Elijah, in 1 Kings 19:9, the Lord talks to him. He said, "Elijah, what are you doing here?" And He commanded him to just step to the very entrance of the cleft—not outside of it, just on the edge. Enough that he would be able to see what was going on outside of the cave but still be protected by the shelter it offered. Once Elijah stepped to the edge of the cleft, the Lord passed him by. As the Lord passed by, there was a large windstorm, a large earthquake, and a large fire. And the Lord was not in any of it. After the fire, there was a small, still voice. There, in the small voice, on the edge of the cleft of the rock, Elijah received his next instructions: to anoint the kings of Syria and Israel and to anoint the Prophet Elisha.

My time in the cleft was much like Elijah's. No, it was not full of natural disasters, but I did continue to experience emotional travesty. In September of 2021, two of my grandparents, my mother-in-law, both of my brothers-in-law, my uncle, and my husband's stepfather were all diagnosed with COVID-19. They all had the Delta variant, and it was horrid. Just days after their initial diagnosis, three of the people diagnosed ended up being hospitalized. My grandfather passed away from the virus, my grandmother was in the hospital for a few days shy of a month, and the inflammatory markers they look at to determine how sick you are were so high for my mother-in-law that they began to prep her arm for the ventilator. She asked them to please not put her on the vent and sent out a group text to ask for specific prayers so that her markers would decrease so they did not have to. I recall the sinking feeling I had when I found out that three of my family members were hospitalized while working, and I immediately left work and drove to the hospital. For hours every single day for nearly two weeks, I drove around the hospital in circles, praying and believing God for a miracle for my family. Although our hearts were broken at the passing of my grandpa, he did receive the ultimate miracle of Heaven—the miracle that we all look forward to one day as believers. My grandmother and mother-in-law both have miraculous testimonies of healing that they experienced through the power of prayer and intercession.

Moving forward to February of 2022, this was the month of LLTK. Donovan and I had spent thousands of dollars on a venue; we had paid for promotion, and we had done all the things we knew how to do to plan, execute, and prepare for a conference. All of the controllable variables were in place. But there was one uncontrolled variable in February, and that was winter weather. Two days before LLTK, an ice storm was predicted. It hit the night before LLTK and left hundreds of people in the county without power. We had no choice but to reschedule this event. Due to the previously booked dates of our speakers, the venue, band members, and many other people involved, we had one option. We had to push the conference back one weekend and do our absolute best to try to re-promote within only a seven-day time frame. A conference that was expected to have anywhere from four to six hundred people in attendance had only approximately seventy-five to one hundred attendees. Although the event was not what it was supposed to be, my team and I dusted off the disappointment. We realized there were a lot of factors at play that were beyond our control and decided to make the next one better. The next opportunity would come sooner than we expected.

In around March of 2022, a friend reached out to me from another town about an hour away from where I live. She stated that her church wanted to host a women's event, but the staff did not have time to put together a conference, and she thought it would be neat if I could bring LLTK to their church. After a few conversations with my team and their church staff, we all agreed to it. This event was held in November of 2022. On the weekend of this conference, it again snowed. This was really bizarre because, in the four days leading up to this event, it was seventy degrees outside. Nonetheless, an event projected to host approximately two hundred people hosted only thirty. I drained—overdrew—our ministry's bank account by eight hundred dollars to pay for this event. It was by the grace of God that the account ended up being covered by someone else before there were any serious repercussions. Because we were expecting a couple hundred people, we thought that we would take up enough offering money to recoup the money we knew we were spending on the event. We did not. Our offering was maybe one hundred dollars. I was disappointed in the loss of finances and the number of people in attendance. I want to be clear that I do not put together LLTK for numbers or money; I do it to impact women in my community. I *really believed* in this conference, and I really felt like I heard the Lord say to put it together, but over the past two conferences, it has become difficult to justify spending thousands of dollars for an event that only a handful of people show up to. At some point, I began to feel like LLTK, not just a conference but a part of my dream, was ineffective. This, on top of the loss of the boys, the loss of friends, pets, and my grandparents, was just too much. This did not feel like a cleft or any sort of safe place. This "cleft" was starting to feel harmful and unsafe. I had a burning urge to get out of "God's safety" as quickly as possible.

NO

From the time that I was a little girl, I dreamed of raising a family and doing ministry with my kids on my hip and my husband by my side. Literally, when my eighth-grade teacher asked what I wanted to do when I grew up, I told her full-time ministry. Her response? "Oh, that does not surprise me at all." When I overdrew my bank account for a conference that dropped from four hundred ladies in attendance to thirty, it felt like God was just saying no to every dream I had. My dream of raising a family, my dream of full-time ministry, and certainly my dream of doing them both at the same time. While it seemed like I was watching my goals dissipate, I was watching God breathe life into everything Donovan set his hands to.

In 2022, Donovan's music ministry blew up almost overnight. No really. In November of 2022, Donovan had four thousand followers on Instagram. By January 1, 2023, Donovan had over ten thousand followers on Instagram. Currently, as I write this in November of 2023, he has one hundred and thirty-five thousand followers on Instagram. Donovan was invited to open for Anne Wilson and Matthew West just this year; he has been getting booking requests to travel all over the United States to sing and testify about Jesus—namely LA, Dallas, Houston, New York City, and Pennsylvania—and that's just to name a few. While these open doors were a sweet answer to Donovan's prayers, it left me feeling disappointed, and defeated, like God's "no" to me was going to be eternal, like I was just going to live life in the shadow of my husband. I felt incredibly vulnerable and emotionally exposed while consecutively feeling tucked away and unseen by the Father. This was certainly a place of obscurity, and it was unlike any season I had ever walked through.

As I walked through this season, or sat down in it, rather, and became unwilling to move, I began to study the story of the

Gentile women. This story can be read in Matthew 15:21–27. While the story of Elijah is forever my favorite Bible story, this one takes a close second. This story is one of my favorites because it ministered to my heart for months as I was hidden away. In this story, this gentile woman comes to Jesus and asks Him to please heal her demon-possessed child. Jesus, at first, does not respond. When I read this scripture, I felt like I was the gentile woman being ignored by Jesus. "Hey Jesus, can you work on the situation with the boys?" *Crickets.* "Hey Jesus, can you teach me how to run a successful women's event, and turn LLTK into more than a conference?" *Silence.* "Hey, God, can you..." *No response.* In His silence, I became frustrated and bitter. I began to ask myself questions like "Is God good?" and "Does God have my best interest in mind?" I would weep before my therapist, my friends, my husband, and my family, and I would say things like "It feels like God has turned His face away from me. Every prayer I prayed regarding the boys, LLTK, you name it, feels like it is going unheard." While all of the people that I groaned to were always supportive and encouraging, that is not everyone's story. Some of you guys reading this have deep grief in your spirit and deep heart wounds. As you try to talk to people in the church, in your friend group, your family, etc., you may not be met with grace and help. It is entirely possible that you are met with people who tell you to stop complaining and keep your frustrations to yourself. They may say things like "You mean to tell me you are not healed from that yet?" or "Oh my gosh, can you get over it already? It has been months." These people remind me of the disciples in this story of the gentile women.

As the woman continued speaking to Jesus, begging Him for an answer, the disciples told Jesus to send her away because she was getting on their nerves. So now, not only has Jesus ignored her when she made her request known to Him, but His friends were annoyed at her request also. Finally, Jesus responded to the woman—His words were not what any of us would like to hear: "I was sent to help the Israelites. Not the Gentiles." He told her no. We can all relate to Jesus telling us no, right? Maybe you are reading, and you feel like you've cried out to Heaven for your heart's desire. Maybe you have struggled with infertility and have begged God to give you a baby. Perhaps your marriage is crumbling, and you have asked God for restoration in your marriage. Maybe you have been living paycheck to paycheck and you have asked God for a financial breakthrough. Perhaps you feel like He is ignoring you, or perhaps you feel like He has moved past ignoring your request. He is simply saying "no."

His "no" did not phase the woman, but as I read this passage of scripture, it did phase me. As a girl who was raised in a nondenominational, charismatic, gentile household, I was taught that the ministry of Jesus was for me. Why did He essentially tell this gentile woman that His ministry was not for her? After many conversations with some very wise people, I learned that it was because He had not gone to the cross yet—the veil had not been torn. It is not that the ministry of Jesus was not for the gentile women; it is solely because the veil had not been torn yet; the time of miracles for the Gentiles was not yet. It is almost like Jesus was not telling the gentile woman, "No." He was telling her, "Not yet." I read this story now, and I imagine Jesus putting the gentile woman in the cleft of the rock—a safe place—while she waited for the timing in which He would begin to work on her behalf.

The Gentile women and I would prove to be two very different types of people. As Jesus placed her in the cleft, she continued to ask Jesus for her desired answer. She pressed into the Father for her need, and He answered her prayer. I had a very different response. My initial response was to remove myself from it. If Jesus was not going to make things happen for me, I would take matters into my own hands. If Jesus would not take me out of this miserable cleft where I felt so unseen and unheard, I was going to remove myself.

OUT OF THE CLEFT TOO EARLY

When my husband and I first got married, I was obsessed with the show *Criminal Minds*. I would binge-watch several episodes a day for months. There was one episode in particular that made me stop watching altogether for a few weeks because it hit a little too close to home. It starts with a girl whose car broke down on the side of the road, and I have been in that situation way too many times to count. The young lady sat in her car, waiting to be rescued. She was in an incredibly wooded area, and there was no cell phone service. As she fumbled with her flip phone, trying to get it to call a family member, it kept showing "no signal." As she wrestled with getting a call to go through, this tow truck pulled up beside her. Fearful of the two men getting out of the truck and wandering to her car, she cranked her window just enough that she could communicate easily with the men on the outside of her car. Hey, guys. Can I help you?" "Help us? Can we help you? You are the one broken down on the side of the road." "Yeah, there's no service here. I'm trying to get hold of my family." "Well, we have a tow truck; we can tow you back to town if you would like. You can pay us when we get you back safely."

You could see the hesitation in her eyes as she got out of her car and into the middle seat of the tow truck. The hesitation in her eyes turned immediately into fear as she realized they were not taking her to town. They were taking her to their house, where they would lock her car in a garage and release her into the vastness of the Oregon woods to try to "run away from them." Once she had been roaming around the forest for several days, they would track her down and hunt her like she was a wild animal. The girl did escape these men, but only because she found a small cleft to hide in on a mountainside she hiked up. There she hid until the men who were seeking to kill her were out of sight. Then, she was able to run to safety. I often wonder what would have happened to the girl in the show had she come out of the cleft a minute earlier than she did, or if she had come out a few minutes later? Would they have been able to track the girl down? Would she have made it to safety? What if she just stayed in the cleft of the rock and waited for someone to find her? Would she have ever been found, or would she have made friends with the cleft and stayed there for eternity?

As the men hunted and tracked the girl from this episode of criminal minds, they walked by the cleft of the rock she was in several times. Had she come out a moment too soon or a moment too late, she would have been found by them. So it is with us as Jesus has us in our cleft—if we come out a moment too soon or a moment too late, it could be detrimental to us. There is a perfect time that God has for our unveiling, and it is dire that we do not miss it. Let's revisit Elijah (again). Had Elijah come completely out of the cleft of the rock before the Lord told him to, he could have been caught up in a natural disaster—the fire, the windstorm, or the earthquake. Elijah waited until just the right time to come out, and, because of that, he heard the still, small voice of God. The voice of God that he heard gave him instructions for where he was to go next. Had he missed it due to his own stubbornness, insecurities, or negative self-talk, he would have missed the next best thing God had for him.

It is believed that this is the very same mountain that Moses was on when he saw the glory of God in Exodus 33:18. In this passage of scripture, Moses asks God to show him His glory. Does this sound like a familiar prayer to you? Glory means magnificence, and our hearts LONG to see God's magnificence in every detail of our lives. When I prayed for restoration in the situation with the boys, when I prayed that God would turn LLTK into something more, I was not just praying for my heart's desires; I was praying for the glory of God to be revealed in my life. In verses 20-23, God tells Moses, "I will show you my glory. But you cannot see me and live. What I will do is place you in the cleft of the rock while my glory passes you by. Then you can see my glory from behind." (This is the paraphrased version.)

There are two things this passage of scripture should teach us. The first thing is that coming out of the safety of the cleft of the rock can be deadly—had Moses looked directly at the face of God, he would have been killed. Dropped dead. He would have never seen the magnificence of God. The second thing we learn here is that we almost always see the glory of God after it has passed us by. When we are in the middle of hard, desolate situations, not only is it hard to recognize that we are in the cleft being protected from something, but we don't realize that being in the cleft is EVIDENCE of God's glory. While Moses was in the cleft of the rock, the **GLORY** of the **MOST HIGH** was **RESTING** upon him; he had absolutely no idea. It was only after he came out of the cleft of the rock that he realized he was surrounded by the glory and magnificence of God. Could it be that even though many of us have been placed in the cleft of the rock, we feel unseen, hidden away, and unheard, like Jesus is ignoring every single one of our prayers, like the church people have disregarded us—that we actually have the glory of God resting upon us? Could it be that the reason we have not "seen the glory" is that we're still in the cleft, and coming out too early could be detrimental to us? Could it be that as you live out this season, and as Jesus starts to answer your prayers and remove you from the cleft, you will realize that the glory of God has passed you by? Perhaps you will see it from behind and know that His hand, His glory, and His magnificence have been in the most obscure, heartbreaking season with you the entire time; you were just not able to recognize it. Could it be that, as you read this even now, you are having a divine revelation that there is a divine appointment for your unveiling that you do not need to miss? Please, do not make friends with your cleft, for the season of being tucked away does not last forever. Also, please do not be so ready to come out of the cleft that you remove yourself before it is time. Listen for that still, small voice that will give you instructions on how to move forward. It is coming. How do I know? Because I, too, have been there. I heard it.

Chapter

8

I AM MY OWN BOSS

It was a warm, sunny day—early September. You could tell that summer was nearing an end, which made me so very sad. I am a summertime girl—I like the feeling of my chunky thighs sticking to the leather in my hot car on a July day; I like swimming, cookouts, and late-night car rides with the windows down. Just the thought of the turn of the season from summer to fall is enough to put me in a bad mood, but it seemed like a bad mood was what I stayed in most of the time anyway, so the change of the seasons in this particular year really made no difference. On this specific day, I had taken the backroads from my job to my nanny's house. I had agreed to stop and help her cut some of the mats out of her very large Great Pyrenees hair very quickly. We had a routine, so it would not take long. I would feed Moose cookies, and she would cut the mats while he was eating—this was no doubt a two-person job.

Normally, I would stay and visit Nanny after helping her with Moose, but on this day, I was in a rush. I had to hurry to pick up Mom and Donovan, which is about ten minutes away from Nan, and then we had to drive to the complete other side of the county to look at a home Donovan and I were considering buying. We had been house-searching for a while, and this seemed to be the perfect home. Downstairs was a fully renovated basement, laundry room, and two decent-sized bedrooms. I could envision it. The basement would be the family room, one of the bedrooms would double as the toy room and my craft room, and the other would serve as Donovan's studio room! This was the perfect start to a house tour. Going up the stairs, you walked into a decent-sized living area and kitchen.

Off to the left of the kitchen was a small hallway that led to four bedrooms. A bedroom for me, and a bedroom for all of the kids we wanted—I wanted—to have. To the right of the kitchen was a sliding door that led to an unfinished deck. Unfinished did not phase me; I was a visionary. We could finish the deck and put a pool at the bottom. A perfect place for our future kids to play on long summer days. Out back, there was a cute little patio. This would be a perfect place to hang some twinkle lights and put up a fire pit. Out back, there was also a garage. Now, Donovan and I are not garage people. We do not work on lawnmowers, or paint trucks, but we do have a ton of storage, and that building would be the perfect place to put it. This house posed no complaints. This was our dream home.

Yet, something was off. It was on the back side of the county. It was a forty-five-minute drive away from my job; it was a twenty-five-minute drive away from my mom; and it was just not what I wanted. But it was what I wanted. It was, and it was not. All at the same time. That is what this season of life looked like for me. After we left, we dropped my mom off to meet my dad at the Mexican restaurant down the road. After she got out of the car, Donovan and I went through the McDonald's drive-through, and we sat in the parking lot of the previously mentioned Mexican restaurant with our drive-through food and talked. Donovan asked me, "What do you want, Kayleigh?" As tears welled up in my eyes, I stated, "I want exactly what I want when I want it. What I want changes from day to day. But I want what I want when I want it." What did that mean? If I got an itch to buy a new pair of Hokas, I wanted to buy them immediately. If I had a desire to get a new iPhone because mine was broken and not "up to par" anymore, I wanted to go to AT&T without hesitation. If I wanted to go to Dairy Queen for ice cream, I wanted to go now—any idea I had, I had without the forethought of patience. Without hesitation, Donovan said, "That is probably the truest statement you have ever made."

It hurt my heart that this was the truth, but it was the reality. I was so exhausted by God's "no." If He was not going to take me out of the cleft of the rock, I was going to take myself out of it, and if

He was not going to breathe life into my current dreams to have kids and do full-time ministry with my husband, I would develop new dreams and breathe life into my *own* dreams. For months, this is what I did. I found a new dream to be skinny (not healthy, skinny), so I changed my primary care physician to a holistic doctor who could help me lose weight—I followed a gluten- and dairy-free diet for six months, per her request. I lost ten pounds in two weeks, and I thought I would start THRIVING. But after those two weeks, I did not lose any more weight. I spent money to hire a virtual personal trainer. I followed his diet and exercise plan for a full two months and honestly saw no additional change. I. Began. To. Spiral. Not only did I gain back the ten pounds I lost, but I also gained an additional thirty. Obviously, being "skinny" was not the way out of the cleft. I blamed my hypothyroidism for that (my lack of hard work could never be the problem). So next, I tried being more intentional with how "put together I was."

Surely, my togetherness would pull me out of this cleft. If my outfits were perfect, my makeup was done, and my hair was in place, people would notice me. I would not be unseen and unheard and unnoticed if I looked the part. I could pull myself out of this place of obscurity. I mean, I notice all of the pretty girls. It made sense that if I looked like them, maybe other people would notice me, too. This lasted all of three months. The intentionality it takes to wake up early, wet and gel your naturally wavy hair so it holds all day, put on a full face of makeup, and pick out an over-the-top outfit is simply way too much to complete before the sun comes up. Do not get me wrong, I love to play in makeup and dress up. I love to gel my naturally curly hair so that it lays beautifully, versus throwing it in a wad on top of my head; I just love to do those things when it is convenient for me. Are you noticing something here? Maybe a pattern? You are seeing a pattern of a girl who wants to do what she wants when she wants to do it. Through trying to pull myself out of the cleft, I learned I did not have the strength or willpower to do so on my own. I also felt as if Jesus had every intention of leaving me there forever. So, now I needed a new way to cope with being in this place of obscurity. I started operation "make friends with the cleft and 'quit' all things that seek to pull you out of that place." The first thing on the chopping block was my ministry, followed by friends who tried pushing me to faith, followed by a husband whose shadow I felt like I lived in.

"NORMAL"

This part of the chapter was probably the hardest for me to write because it is how this book started. This is where most of the inspiration for *Becoming Her* comes from. When I was struggling with depression, I was not thinking about who I was called to be or how to accomplish my purpose. I was only thinking about how I would survive the day. But, while in this cleft, I was not depressed; I ended up becoming fiercely content. I have an excellent job that I love very much. I have a house that feels like home next to my mom. We may or may not consider buying it, and I am okay with either. I have a dog that I love dearly and three cats that annoy me greatly, but still, they bring joy to my life. Life feels "mostly normal."

We go to church, and we eat lunch with family after church. Sunday afternoons usually consist of grocery shopping, meal-prepping our food for the week, taking a nap or swimming, watching a movie, or doing some sort of fun activity to wrap up the weekend. We work Monday to Friday, we enjoy our Saturdays, and on Sundays, we do it all again. It is a very "normal," regular life, and it is comfortable. I do, however, often find myself questioning how I went from this zealous girl who beat depression, the girl who would imagine herself dressed like Katniss Everdeen coming out of the darkest pit, ready to take on life's hardest tasks, to this new girl—this girl who thrives in the normalcy of what society teaches the American Dream is. I am certainly not trying to scorn people who have built their version of the American dream and are proud to be living their dream, but normal was never my dream. I never wanted the big house on the hill with the white picket fence. I always wanted to do full-time ministry, to follow Jesus down whatever path He was leading me down. Down the path of marriage, having kids, fostering kids, pastoring, or hosting events—whatever serving our communities and the communities of our friends and families looked like—that is what I wanted to do. But now, I just want God to stop telling me "no."

In an effort to silence His "no," I began to silence my belief for things, and I began to silence the people in my life who had faith to believe for things. The first thing I silenced was my belief in God for women's ministry. Love Like the King was a yearly conference that took place in February. I was so afraid that the next conference would not be well attended like the previous two that I decided not to do LLTK anymore. People would say, "Kayleigh, don't you mean you want to postpone it?" No. I did not mean that. I meant that I did not want to do it anymore. I was tired of losing money. I was tired of feeling like I was not having an impact on women in my area. I was just done. Per Donovan's request, we rescheduled it. Per my request, it got rescheduled four times because I was not ready to take on another conference. I was comfortable in the cleft, and LLTK was going to screw up my comfort zone. No way was I going to purposely mess up my own peace and comfort.

After I silenced my belief for women's ministry, I silenced my desire for other kinds of ministry, too. I stopped wanting to help Donovan with his music ministry. I mean, I would still work his merch table at shows that I attended with him, but I did not attend very many shows. I hated when he would talk to me about his music. It honestly felt like a brag to me. He would come home from work and say, "I got an email from the Brooklyn Nets to come perform for their G-League Half Time Show in NYC," or "Baby, a church from Dallas invited me to their youth event," or "Marty from social club wants me to meet him in Nashville to introduce me to some people." And while it was all excellent things, it was like God was breathing on every single avenue Donovan walked down, and I was just ... in the cleft. I was mad at Donovan for God breathing on his dream, mad at God for not breathing on any of mine. So I just stopped caring about Donovan's ministry. God was caring enough for both of us.

This led to friction in my marriage beyond anything that we had previously experienced. I mean, yes, the first three years of marriage were a living nightmare, but this was a different kind of warfare. This was spiritual warfare, but Donovan was the only one fighting the enemy. I was just fighting him. Because I was ready to lay down ministry due to my own past hurt and frustrations, I was ready for him to lay it down, too. Our arguments frequently sounded like this: "Donovan, why can't you just stop doing music? This is crazy. It is causing so much friction in our marriage." He would say, "Kayleigh, this is my dream. God made me for this. What about the stuff you used to say God made you for? Why don't you want to do that anymore?" And I would say, "I just want to be normal. Normal people do not do women's conferences; they do not travel or do music. They go to work, then come home. They go to the beach once a year. They have kids. They take their kids to Disney World. Why can't that be enough for you?" He would respond, "Why is it good enough for you? You do not believe God for anything anymore."

These conversations happened a lot and usually ended with him upset and me throwing around the "D" word because, in my mind, divorce was certainly easier than relinquishing my pride and succumbing to the reality that Donovan was right about my unbelief in Jesus. And certainly, I did not want to give God the opportunity to heal the broken parts of my heart that were still tucked away in the cleft. Because, well, in all honesty, I was holding God responsible for the hurt in my heart. It was God's fault that we lost the boys. It was God's fault that it snowed both weekends of the previous LLTKs and no one showed up. I mean, there has to be someone to blame, right? And it could not be my lack of hard work or the sinful nature of man, or that we live in a fallen world and sometimes unfortunate things just happen, and God teaches us to trust Him through it, could it? No. It had to be solely God's fault to make myself feel better about this new "normal"—a life without the pursuit of the Father—that I was dead set on living.

Other than just ministry, I stopped believing God to answer other prayers too. I stopped praying that we would have kids. I even stopped wanting kids. I stopped praying over our finances. When people would ask me questions, I presented the answer as this very holy place of contentment. I would say, "I am just content with where the Lord has me," or "Ya know, if we never have kids, or never buy a house, or never have our ministry dreams come to fruition, I want to be okay with just Jesus." While I was content with not buying this house, not having kids, or not doing ministry, it was not because of this place of contentment with the Lord. It was solely because I was so tired of God telling me no to past prayers, hopes, and dreams. What if I prayed for kids and prayed over finances? What if I stepped out of the cleft and began to dream again, and God said "no" again? That would just crush me. I was finally content with God's "no," and I decided that I would rather not have the things I really want out of life than put my faith out there again and potentially believe Him for an answer that is never coming.

ANOINTING COMES WITH A COST

In December of 2022, I joined this Bible study group with six other women. We started reading this amazing book called Five Habits of a Woman Who Doesn't Quit by a phenomenal lady named Nicki

Koziarz. In the very first chapter of the book, I learned that I have almost every single trait of a quitter. This should come as no surprise to you since you have just read stories in this very book about how I tried to quit marriage several times. In the paragraphs just above this one, you read about how I tried to quit ministry and convince Donovan to do so as well. In fact, just days after we started reading Five Habits of a Woman Who Doesn't Quit, I told my Bible study group that I wished God would uncall me. You have read about how I quit my faith, but no, these are just the things I have tried to quit in the last twelve months. Throughout my life, I have quit every single sport I have played; I have quit friends; I have quit health plans and exercise classes; and had I not been afraid of dying, I would have quit living. Through life, I became acquainted with the reality that quitting is simply easier than developing the tenacity to push forward.

Throughout my season of being in the cleft, I became acutely aware of this unfortunate reality that to become all that God has created me to be, there is a process that I am constantly required to work through. To become a pastor, to be a leader of men, there is heartbreak you have to endure, and trials you have to persevere through. These trials are not just one-and-done. They come. Then they come again. Then again and again and again. I desired to quit my faith simply because I was tired of the trials. I thought the church hurt and the depression was enough of a trial. And then, I thought surely, the loss of the boys would be enough. I thought maybe, eventually, I would not have to keep doing grossly hard things. And then I encountered the loss of the expectation of what I thought LLTK was going to be, while consecutively losing close friends and pets. Reality started to set in that to become the future version of me—the me that God wants me to be—there is a lot of processing that has to take place, and, unfortunately, the processing is not going to stop until we are in Heaven with the Father, or we are completely like Christ. Simply put, I did not want to be processed anymore. I decided that I would forego the calling of God if it meant the present pain would stop. This is where I found myself. Normal. Refusing to become her.

*If you want the anointing, expect to be crushed
because the oil comes from the crushing.*
—UNKNOWN

If you have ever listened to a sermon by Jentezen Franklin, TD Jakes, Christine Caine, or any Christian speaker of influence, they have all preached a similar sermon or said a similar quote to the one shared above. This is because, throughout the entire Bible, literally all the way from the Old Testament to the New Testament, oil was used to anoint God's people; if you have ever been to a modern Christian church, you have probably either had someone dab a dot of oil on your forehead in the prayer line, or you have maybe at the very least seen a container of oil laying around the pastor's pulpit for anointing purposes. This practice of "anointing" is still used today. The original intent of anointing a person was to sanctify them, or to mark them as "set apart as holy." Of course, kings and priests were "anointed" by people, but there were people, like Jesus, whom God anointed Himself—not with physical oil, but with spiritual oil—oil that no one can see. In Luke 4:18 ESV, Jesus states, "The spirit of the Lord is upon me because he has anointed me to proclaim good news to the poor ..." 1 John 2:20 tells us that we have an anointing from Jesus, through His death and resurrection.

Anointing is what many of us pray for. When we think of anointing, we think of Paul, Jesus, and Peter, the men that demons recognized—at least I do. I am reminded of when, in Acts 16, Paul and Silas were WALKING TO PRAYER. They were minding their own business and going about their own duties when this demon-possessed girl came up behind them. She began mocking them. At first, Paul did nothing. He said nothing. But the demon in this girl mocked and taunted Paul and Silas for literal days, according to the scripture, and it got on Paul's nerves. So he just commanded the demon to leave. I think of another time when these Jewish men were casting demons out in the "Name of Jesus whom Paul preaches." Literally, one of the demons that these self-acclaimed exorcists, as the New King James Version calls them, was trying to cast out responded. It said, "Paul I know. And Jesus I know. But who are you?" Ahhh, to be known by hell, right? We chatted about that earlier in this book. To be recognized by the enemy as a "troubler of Israel." The anointing Paul and Jesus walked in? We crave it. We pray for it. We fast for it. But we rarely realize it comes with a cost.

Olive oil is the oil that was traditionally used to anoint people, so I watched a video on how olive oil is made. When olives are harvested, they are harvested by a very large machine that has the capacity to wrap its arms around the tree. The machine will give the tree a very forceful shaking until all of the olives have fallen off of the tree. Next, the olives are sent for cleansing so that anything that was caught up with the olives during harvesting that is not needed for the oil itself can be washed away. In the original method, before the recent modernization of factories and updated machinery, the olives were then crushed by being pushed through a grinder and made into a pulp. This pulp was then packed into this giant pancake-like structure and then sent into another part of a factory, where the pulp in the pancake-like structure was literally pressed until this purified oil was squeezed out. Certainly, if we wish to ooze pure oil—the type of anointing that casts out demons simply because they are getting on our nerves and the type of anointing that gets us recognized as a troubler of Israel—we will endure things that will shake us. We will be forced to be cleansed. We may feel like we are being crushed. We will be pressed from all sides. And then? We will ooze pure oil—undefiled anointing. No, this is not a glorious process, but the end result is often something we pray for.

I heard this quote once. Originally, it was said by Dietrich Bonhoeffer, but I heard Pastor Paul from the Belonging in Nashville say it at their conference a few days after my grandfather passed in 2021. "When God calls a man, He bids him to come and die." I think there is a lot of confusion about what that means. When I first heard that, my mind first went to the martyrs—those who have actually given up their physical lives for the Gospel. And maybe it could mean that in a sense, but more than that, it means we have to be willing to be crucified daily to carry the weight of anointing. Even as I type this, I can hear the echoes of God in my spirit saying, "Oh yeah. I will allow you to perform miracles, but you have to start fasting." "Oh yeah, I will allow you to prophesy, but you have to get that smart mouth under control." "Absolutely, you can lead worship. But first, you have to learn to serve your husband." "Sure, you can be a pastor, start a church, or grow a ministry, but first you have to learn to care about someone other than yourself."

As Americans, we are so accustomed to everything being fast. We have fast food, fast cars, and fast money; everything in this country is so sped up. We often want the right now gratification of the power of anointing without the processing of God, and I am not excluded from that. I cannot count the times I have prayed that God would remove me from the season of feeling like loss surrounds me. After we lost the boys, there was an ache and a disappointment that was in my heart almost constantly. There were days when I felt genuinely abandoned by God—like He did not even care to turn His ear toward me as I bitterly wept. I do not have enough fingers and toes to show for the amount of times I have sobbed before the Lord, before Donovan, before my therapist, my mom, my best friend—my greatest mentors. I expressed to them the desire that I had to be "regular," and I told some of them how I felt abandoned by God. I even told a couple of them how because I was in a place of no longer wanting to do ministry because of the hurt in my heart, I also wanted Donovan to lay down the things God has called him to do and be "regular" with me. If there had ever been a season in which God had bid me to come and die, it was this one. No, it was not the one where I was depressed and my marriage sucked, and I was so broke that I was receiving government assistance. It was not when I was crying over some terrible things people from church said to me. It was the one where my home felt empty and all of God's promises seemed like they were going unfulfilled in my life. Being anointed by Heaven and known by hell sounded amazing to me in my early twenties. The idea that Satan feared me was one that got my wheels turning when my alarm went off in the mornings—and then I found myself in a place where I would have rather laid down every promise I ever prayed for just so hell would leave me alone.

I understand what "becoming her" will take. I have spent enough time in church listening to the sermons about how olive oil—how anointing—is made; I have spent time with anointed people and heard their stories of pain. I know that it will cost me something to become her. It will cost me more processing, more heartache, more weeping before the Lord, more feeling abandoned, more friends leaving, and more betrayal. And as I was in the season of making besties with my cleft, I was unsure that I wanted that. I found myself stuck in this process of choosing between staying who I currently am—the girl who will live a decent life and spend eternity with Jesus—or the girl I am called to be—the one who will make an impact on her generation.

I started writing this portion of the book in January of 2023, and I had to go back and change some of the verbiage here because I have made a decision on which way I lean. It is November of 2023 now, and I sometimes still find myself standing in this valley of decision. When I do, I always look to Jesus through scripture. Jesus is always presented as the Savior, the Healer, and the Miracle Worker, but rarely is His suffering talked about—rarely is any suffering talked about in the body of Christ, yet throughout scripture, many of God's people suffered. I think about how Jonah must have felt as he sat in the belly of a fish for three days, wondering how painful his death would be. He could not have expected that he would be spit up on the shore of his destiny a few days later. I wonder how Daniel felt as he was thrown into a lion's den and if Shadrach, Meshach, and Abednego were afraid when they realized they were going to be tossed into a fiery furnace like yesterday's garbage. I think about Joseph and how he was sold into slavery by his brothers, how Hannah felt like she was being taunted by the enemy for not being able to conceive, and how she wept before the Lord in the Tabernacle. In the New Testament, John the Baptist was beheaded, Paul and Peter were arrested, and they attempted to murder Paul many times before succeeding. And Jesus, He was no stranger to suffering.

In Matthew 26:36, Jesus goes into the Garden of Gethsemane to pray. He brings Peter, James, and John along with Him and asks them to pray, too. He tells them that His soul is crushed with grief to the point of death. Luke 22 explains that Jesus, as he was praying, His soul was in such agony that He was actually sweating blood. This man was beyond anxious. There is not a word in the English language to express the anguish He was in as He prayed, begging God that the cup of suffering that was going to be passed to Him could be taken. He knew that He was going to be beaten, and mocked, that His clothes would be ripped off of His body and gambled for. He knew that nine-inch nails were going to be hammered into His hands, that when His body was the weakest it had ever been, He would be forced to carry a cross uphill and get hit with a whip and chastised the whole way. He knew that when He asked for a drink of water on the cross as He was gasping for air, the soldiers who wanted Him dead would give him vinegar, and He knew that they would pierce His side as He hung there.

As Jesus was praying in the Garden, there are three things He said that inspire me as I stand in my own personal valley of decision regarding who I am now, and who I am called to be. He says twice in Matthew 26:39, "My Father! If it is possible, let this cup of suffering be taken away from me …" referencing the things He was going to have to endure in the days to come. "… Yet I want your will to be done, not mine." Then, in Matthew 26:41, He says, "… the spirit is willing, but the body is weak!" Both of these things have inspired me, even in the past two weeks, as I have wept on my way to work in the mornings as I worshiped and prayed, sobbed in my office before my work day began as I let the love of Jesus wash over me, and even spent some time crying in worship in my car on my lunch break. It is inspirational to me because, **EVEN THOUGH** I have warred with wanting God to uncall me, the purity of my heart is that God would use me and that His will would be done in my life. **EVEN THOUGH** my face has been downcast and my heart has been broken, my spirit is willing to do the hard things—to go through unrelenting trial after trial, process after process—anything to become the version of me that is living out her calling and purpose to its fullest extent.

The last thing Jesus did that really blessed my heart as I read this chapter and inspired me on my own journey can be found in Matthew 26:50. It is when Jesus is about to get arrested in the Garden and Judas, His betrayer, walks up to Him and kisses Him on the cheek. Jesus says, "Go ahead and do what you have come for." In the very next part of the story, we see Peter ready to fight the people who came to arrest Jesus—he even cuts one of the dudes' ears off. Jesus picks the man's ear up, puts it back on his face, and basically says to Peter (paraphrasing), "Hey Peter. I could have legions of angels rescue me from this if I ask. But then how would the scriptures be fulfilled if I were to do that?"

"Becoming her" will require me to go through more heartbreak. It will require me to go through more processing, more betrayal, and more loss. I could almost vomit at the thought of having to experience more of anything negative. But the reality is that, when all is said and done, I deeply desire to be like Jesus. I *could* choose "normal." I *could* choose to lay down my faith and stop the pursuit of the Father at the arrival of the next trial. I *could* lay down my desire to "become her." I have done it in the past. But I will try to never choose those things again. Walking through hard circumstances and deep sorrow will not just make me more like Him, but it will strengthen my walk with Him.

Also, the things I have learned in my journey are things that I now want to share with you. Do you get it? Jesus gave my story a voice, and He wants to do the same with you. We are not on a mission to become who God created us to be, so we can be silent about our redemption. God is in the process of clefting us so He can mold us. Once we are molded, He will unveil us so He can release us to tell of His goodness and faithfulness to us in a time when we wondered if He was even present. Rejoice as you read this, and no, do not be downcast. Please be assured that God wastes nothing. The season that you are in is not in vain, and there is a time coming for God to reveal His glory in your life in a way that you have never experienced—perhaps it will be in a way that you did not expect. His glory revelation, however, will show up in a way that stirs your faith and reminds you that not only does God see you, but He has seen you the whole time—even when you thought you were tucked away in obscurity.

Chapter

9

PHYSICAL RETREAT AND SPIRITUAL ALARMS

At the very beginning of this book, I briefly mentioned how, at a retreat, I spoke to a girl named Alyssa, who told me she could listen to me talk all day. She told me those words in September of 2022, and a whole year later, in September of 2023, I was speaking at that same retreat again. Not a lot had changed in that year, only a few things. I was still in the "cleft," I was still feeling unseen by God, and I was still debating his goodness on a regular basis. But starting in January of 2023, the Lord asked me to spend a year off of social media to heal, to focus, and to listen for His whisper. You know, like the one that Elijah heard as he was coming out of the cleft. I thought for sure taking the time off of social media like God had asked would be just the thing to pull me out of the three-year funk I had been in. I was wrong. It was September of 2023; it had been nine months of "healing, focusing, and listening for a whisper from Heaven," and it felt like the intentionality of silencing my notifications per **HIS REQUEST** did not matter. He, too, had been silent. I had no idea that going into a retreat I was asked to speak at would be the start of a wake-up call that would not only begin to sound alarms in my spirit but one that would stir my soul to encourage others to not press snooze on the alarms that may be sounding in theirs.

The retreat would take place, from Friday to Sunday, with girls arriving as early as 5 p.m. on Friday. Friday, which would be night one of this retreat, was really regular. I almost stayed home, actually, because I knew that it would be "regular." There were no Bible studies taking place on this night, no group talks taking place. It was going to be a slumber party with snacks, games, and karaoke, and while I knew it would be fun, leaving home for me in this season was hard. In the months and weeks leading up to the retreat, Donovan had some health issues pop up. Just a week before the retreat, Donovan had a lymph node removal surgery to test for lymphoma. Along with an armpit full of stitches, Donovan had a drain tube coming from his incision site. Despite the fact that I had agreed to be at this retreat—matter of fact, we both had—before any of these health issues arose, and although Donovan was going to be there on Sunday for us to give the marriage talk together, I just did not want to go. In lieu of the surgery, and honestly, the fear of a cancer diagnosis, I just wanted to be with my husband. Leaving him for any number of minutes made my chest hurt and caused my anxiety to soar. Regardless of my feelings, I did go to the retreat on that Friday night. Donovan kind of forced me, but it was good to go early and get my mind off of things. We also felt that regardless of my personal matters, I needed to carry out the duties of my commitments.

Night one was filled with loud laughter and sweet giggles. We sang karaoke to the Cheetah Girls and Taylor Swift, ate more pizza than necessary, and stayed up all night chatting with old and new friends. It was truly a blast. Then came day two. This is the day those alarm bells started to sound in my spirit. Day two was filled with testimonies and vulnerable talks. As women told of the seasons of life they were in, almost every single one of them said something similar to "God has me in a season that I absolutely hate. And if I could choose not to walk through this, I would." Or, "I do not like where God has me. I feel unseen. I feel like all of my prayers have fallen on deaf ears." One by one, as women got up to tell their testimonies, very few of them testified about a season God brought them out of. They shared about the season they were currently in. A season that they did not like, one that was unfamiliar, and lonely, one that they desperately wished God would remove them from. A season in which they were struggling to find the goodness of God. One by one, as each woman shared about her season, I found myself feeling like I was looking in a mirror. For nearly three years, I had kept all of these thoughts and feelings mostly to myself for fear of judgment. *What would people think when I told them that I hate the season that God has me in? What will they say when I tell them how it's affecting my marriage? How will they respond when they find out that I do not think God is good all the time?* Surely, if the six ladies sharing talks this weekend felt this way, too, we are not the only ones. There are others.

Through conversations throughout the weekend, God began to give me my next instructions. I was finally starting to hear that whisper from God that I had desperately awaited for the last nine months. God was finally nudging me out of the cleft and starting to give me instructions regarding my next steps. He was showing me that I needed to be vulnerable, that I needed to talk to girls who are like me. The ones who feel like they cannot "become her," or the ones who have decided that they do not want to "become her" anymore because she seemed too unattainable. After spending the last year wanting to give up on my ministry dreams to be "normal, this retreat definitely woke me up. My alarms were sounding, and I was dreaming again of all the ways I could reach women who were "like me," but I was not fully awake; I was still "pressing snooze," so to speak. It is easy to come home from a weekend encountering Jesus and slip back into your version of normal, which is exactly what I did. I had no way of knowing what was to come next, but the Lord was definitely going to have my full attention.

FULLY AWAKE

Three weeks after the retreat, on October 6th of 2023, Donovan and I were at lunch. I got off work early, like I do on Fridays, and we met for lunch at the Mexican restaurant. Although not my favorite lunch spot, it is Donovan's favorite, and it had been a while since we had been there together. We went to lunch expecting a normal rest of the weekend, whatever that looked like. Donovan had a show that night, but other than that, not really a lot was going on. It was at this restaurant that Donovan received a notification on his phone that his MyChart had been updated. We had been waiting on his biopsy results for several weeks now, and this was what we had been waiting for. The words on the screen knocked the breath out of me: Follicular T-cell lymphoma. I felt like someone punched me in the gut with a baseball bat. A large lump developed in my throat, and I could feel my eyes begin to water. I felt many emotions and feelings very quickly, most of them negative. Fear. Sadness. Disappointment. Frustration. Just to name a few. While we knew they were testing for cancer, we certainly did not expect them to find it.

I had a choice. I could crawl back into the cleft. Cry. Weep. Question God. And I could stay there forever, wondering why God keeps allowing me to face hard battles that I do not feel equipped to fight. I could give up on the dreams I was dreaming three weeks ago after leaving that retreat, the ones about reaching women like me. I have done all of those things before. I did it when I lost the boys. I did it when I suffered hurt at the hands of fellow church members. I was no stranger to tucking away and hiding when things were tough. But this? Cancer? My husband's health? No. This was an attack by the enemy. I decided while sitting at a green, boothed table at a Mexican restaurant, with tears in my eyes and a lump in my throat, that I and the enemy would go to war. I was going to go to war for the health of my husband.

The seven days following my husband's diagnosis were some of the best and worst days. They were the worst because my anxiety was through the roof. I learned early on—literally by hour three of receiving the diagnosis—that Google was going to be my worst enemy. I set a timer on my Safari to limit myself to ten minutes of Safari screen time a day. This forced me to limit what I was researching. Also, I deleted every social media app and cut out all secular music. Not that Facebook and secular songs are necessarily bad, but my mind was running rampant with thoughts of death.

My flesh was weak. I was afraid of the future. I was afraid to pray for healing for Donovan; afraid God would choose not to heal him. I was scared that again I would be left feeling unseen, unheard, and utterly heartbroken by the Father. My fear of his diagnosis was overpowering my faith in Jesus, so it became necessary that I cut out anything that did not lead me to the heart of the Father. I even began to fast. For four days, I did not touch a single bite to eat. These decisions that I made—to fast, to delete apps, and to set timers on screen time—these are all things that led me closer to Jesus. These are all decisions that led me to some of the best days—days where my faith was getting stronger; days that I could finally start to taste freedom.

The week and weekend after we received Donovan's diagnosis was a week and weekend filled with every emotion. I remember the Monday following his diagnosis, sitting in my office at work. My laptop was broken, I was twisting my hair, playing worship music on my phone, and waiting for the IT guy to show up to fix the problem with my laptop. I was also praying. Thinking. Facing the reality that I had wasted the past two years of my life telling God about all of the things I no longer wanted. I was content to give up my marriage, content to not have kids, content to give up anything and everything that would convince the enemy to leave me alone; he still was bothersome. Like a ton of bricks, the magnitude of what I really wanted—all of the things I had been running from for so long hit me. As tears streamed down my face, joy filled my soul. I began to sob words of repentance: "Jesus, I am so sorry for not wanting your best for me. I am sorry for thinking I know best. I am so sorry for being willing to lay You down for comfort. To not have kids. To not pursue my calling. Jesus, I want my marriage. I want to love my husband and serve him and his ministry well. I want to love him and You well with him. Jesus, I want to be a mom, to create a legacy with Donovan, with You at the center. Jesus, I want to do ministry. I want to serve your people. The ones you love.

With babies on my hip and my husband by my side. This is what I was created for. Jesus. I'm sorry I lost sight. Help me to find You here. Help me not to lose sight in this season but to fight for Your purpose for me. For us. For our futures. Help me to believe that you are a good, faithful Father who has Your hand in this." Jesus certainly met me that day in my office. I was fully awake.

FINALLY FREE

The weekend after Donovan's diagnosis just happened to be our anniversary weekend. Donovan had been invited (months before we found out about his diagnosis) to perform at a youth conference in Michigan. It was with great hesitancy that I went. I was annoyed that *this* was how we were going to spend our anniversary. We were going to church, and then we were coming home to oncology appointments and chemotherapy. I had spent the last week in prayer. I had spent the last week fasting. I had spent the last week being awakened to the presence of God and re-learning to trust in a God who performs miracles. But there were still parts of my heart that felt unseen by Heaven. There were still parts of me that wondered if God *actually heard* me, or if He *actually saw* me. Centreville, Michigan, was a six-and-a-half-hour drive, so I would have plenty of time to ponder my thoughts. Despite my hesitancy, I was not going to miss this weekend with Donovan. After all, it was the last weekend we were going to have before treatment started.

Once we got to Michigan, we pulled into a cute, quaint, quiet neighborhood, much like the one I grew up in. Strangely, it felt like home. As we walked into our Airbnb, there were homey signs featuring scriptures all over the walls. There was a lovely couch and the most adorable breakfast nook that I had ever seen. The house had an endearing fifties vibe that was so fun and inviting. As we came in and sat our travel bags down in the bedroom, we noticed on the desk near the window this very large bag of snacks.

These were not just regular snacks, like Cheetos and Sour Patch Gummies. These snacks were what we, in rural America, would call the good snacks. These do not come from Walmart—no, these are the ones that come from a Whole Foods, or a Trader Joe's. We had multiple kinds of pita chips, chocolate-covered almonds, different kinds of organic beef jerky, pistachios, and the list goes on and on. I was blown away by the bag of snacks, but underneath that was a card from the ministry that had invited us in. This card was a traditional thank-you card that thanked us for coming to take part in their youth weekend, but this card also featured an honorarium for Donovan. Donovan does not always charge to go to events, and, in this case, he did not. The guy that invited Donovan in, Brenno, was Donovan's music friend. The two have featured together, and this was just going to be a weekend of hanging out with Brenno, and his wife Giulyana, and serving Jesus together.

While the snacks and the honorarium were enough to bless us, Brenno and Giulyana did not stop there. Next to the bag of snacks, there was a gold and white balloon that said "Happy Anniversary" on it. The balloon was being held down by a card in a gold envelope. Once we opened the envelope, a hundred dollars fell out, and written in the card was a sweet anniversary note from Brenno and Giulyana. I was beyond blessed by this point; I was absolutely blown away by their kindness. They had never met us before and they were so kind. Next to the desk, was a green gift bag with golden tissue paper in it that grabbed my attention. I proceeded to open it, and In the bag were two sweatshirts, one purple and one green, both saying, "Kingdom Mindset," and two mint green tee shirts, both saying "Finally Free." These were pieces of Brenno's merch that he and Giulyana were giving to Donovan and me. I said, "Donovan, why did they give us all this stuff?" He said, "I have no idea. I did not know they were doing all of that." To say that we were surprised by their generosity would be an understatement.

After we got settled, Brenno called Donovan and said, "Hey man. Giulyana and I are heading to pick y'all up. We're gonna take y'all to Applebee's. Is that cool?" Donovan and I, hungry from the six-and-a-half-hour drive, were ready to eat, but we were also ready to spend time with the people who were being so kind to us! Donovan had previously met Brenno in Atlanta when he went down for a show, but most of their interactions had been through social media, phone calls, and texts. This was going to be their first time really hanging out, and I had never met either Brenno or his wife; I was very excited! After sitting and chatting for a while, to our surprise, these strangers, who had already given us so much, paid for our dinner, too! After dinner, Brenno drove us back to our Airbnb and informed us that someone would be there to pick us up for breakfast around nine the next morning. We really appreciated the gesture, but we vouched that we'd take ourselves to breakfast. I mean, we had been in their town for less than three hours, and they had already done so much. Nothing else was necessary. Through conversation, we came to a happy medium. Instead of being picked up at our Airbnb, the plan was that the following morning we would drive ourselves to the church around the time the youth conference was getting started. Brenno would introduce us to his leadership team, and there we would meet up with a gentleman named Ryan. Ryan would take us to breakfast, and then we would come back to the conference.

The next morning, we woke up late, as usual, and scrambled to get ready. I threw on one of the new "Finally Free" shirts that Brenno and Giulyana had gifted us. Of course, I brought my own clothes, but who could refrain from wearing new ones? And these shirts were so cute! We drove to the church, and our hosts introduced us to about thirty people in less than five minutes. Our morning was full of hugs and handshakes—and then breakfast with Ryan. Ryan drove us to a spot close to the church called Yoders. This was an Amish spot where everything was cooked homemade every morning. The biscuits and gravy tasted like the kind you'd eat at your granny's house, and the homemade snacks that were for sale there were some of the best I have ever had. After breakfast, it was back to the church to sit in on the youth conference. That morning they had worship, followed by a short talk/call to action, given by Brenno. During this talk, Brenno asked the students how many alarms they had to set to get up in the morning. He mentioned that some people are two alarm people, some are five alarm people, and some are more than that. He then posed the question, "How many times do you press snooze on your alarms before it's too many times?" And then he said, "How many times do you have to press snooze before you get up?" Brenno expressed to the youth that there is a sense of urgency on the Earth for the Gospel to go forth. He discussed things happening in politics, Israel, Hamas, and just all over. You could see that the world needs Jesus more than ever. He asked them if they were waking up to the urgency of becoming who God created them to be or if they were pressing snooze.

As these words rolled off of his tongue, my mouth opened so wide that it could have touched the floor. This was almost verbatim— the exact conversation I and Jesus were having in my office that past Monday. Only, politics and world news were not my wake-up call—mine was cancer. When you are faced with the reality of the fragility of life, you realize you do not want to waste it pleasing one's own self. I realized that day in my office, and I encountered that same realization again as Brenno was speaking, that I only wanted what God wanted. And I believe that God wants me to be a mom, to serve Donovan's ministry, and to do ministry myself. If you had asked me ten years ago what my God dream was, I would have said, 'To do ministry with my husband and my babies on my hip." Cancer re-awoke me to the reality of that dream and to the urgency of accomplishing it. As Brenno spoke, I started to realize that this weekend in small town Michigan was much more than

Brenno and Giulyana being intentional. Jesus was planning to meet me in Michigan that weekend, and I had absolutely no idea.

Midway through the conference, Brenno and his wife's team took the youth leaders upstairs to have a breakout session with them while the youth had breakout sessions downstairs. While Donovan and I were not youth leaders, we stayed in the mini-session with our friends and the handful of people we had met earlier that morning. After the session, Brenno came to Donovan and asked him if he could be a part of the panel for the next part of the youth conference downstairs. He informed Donovan that a member of their church passed away unexpectedly, and many of the members of the panel are going to the wake and will not be in attendance. Donovan agreed but asked that I be on the panel. Brenno had not had many interactions with me; he had no idea that I felt called to preach. Although he looked confused, like he was wondering what I could offer on the panel, he agreed. Some of the questions were hard, but being on that panel was so fun! It had been almost a year since I had gotten to exercise that gift of speaking, solely because God had me in a season of silence. Once the panel was over, Donovan and Brenno both told me that I did an amazing job, which was a compliment from Donovan because he is always a critic, and it seemed to be a compliment from Brenno.

After the panel, Donovan and I left the church and headed back to our Airbnb for a snack and a nap. We knew we had to be back at the church in a few hours for the soundcheck, the setup of Don Ready's merch table, and the performance. The performance from Donovan was incredible. The crowd interaction was amazing, which made the show more entertaining to watch, and, of course, he had a great time! While the show was great, it was the events that took place after that that I still think about. I met Brenno's music producer and his wife. Alicia is her name, and she is probably one of the most genuine, open-book people I have ever encountered. As she shared with me about the season God had her family in, tears began to fill my eyes. It felt like I was talking to myself. I had never met someone who identified completely with the place that I was in spiritually. Our conversation was cut short that night because people had flights they had to catch. and the church needed to be cleaned and put back for the following morning's service, but thankfully, we would have an opportunity to connect again before the weekend was brought to a close.

Once everything at the church was settled, and together, a group of us went to Applebee's for a late-night dinner and to hang out with one of the performing artists the church had brought in. Miles Minnick. I had never met Miles, but he and Donovan had met through social media. They, too, had a couple of songs together, but this was their first time meeting in person. The group that went out to eat that night was Donovan, Brenno, Giulyana, Miles, Miles' manager Jorge, and Brenno's friend Eli. While some of the musicians at the table talked about the future of the industry, I talked to Eli. I have not mentioned Eli in this story yet, but he is one of the youth leaders who helped organize the youth conference. Earlier that day, while at the event, I had been introduced to Eli's wife, Leora, and his nine-week-old baby girl. I love babies, and I so desperately wanted to hold his baby girl at the event. That being said, I do understand the dynamic between newborn babies, germs, and strangers—even strangers who love the Lord and are in a supervised church setting—and I refrained from asking Leora if I could. However, that night at Applebee's, as I was talking to Eli, it came up that I almost asked Leora if I could hold their baby at the event. I listed to him all of the reasons I did not ask (the exact ones listed above). To my surprise, Eli said, "Well, we are not those kinds of parents. She would have definitely let you hold our baby." "I said, "Oh, well. Maybe next time," and did not think anything else of it.

The conversation continued at the dinner table; the server brought our food; we ate; we laughed; and in the middle of eating, out of nowhere, Miles pushed his plate away and began to look unsettled. I say unsettled because that is the only way to describe it, but he was sitting in a way that suggested that he was definitely feeling the Holy Spirit move upon his heart. A holy hush came over the table as we all started to realize that God came to sit down at Applebee's with us. Miles began to prophesy. First, he prophesied to Brenno and Giulyana, and I deeply wish that I remembered the words he spoke to them. After that, he began to prophesy to Donovan. He prophesied to Donovan about finances and about how God would use him as a leader, but then he began to prophesy to Donovan about healing in his body. Immediately, I began to weep. This man had absolutely no idea that just seven days ago we received a diagnosis that would forever change how we carry our faith. My tears were not tears of sorrow, but tears of joy. I began to realize that God was hearing our prayers and our requests for healing. Through a strange man who lives on the complete other side of the country from us—a man whom Donovan occasionally does music with—was a confirmation that there was an answer coming—an answer of healing.

We said our goodbyes to Miles; we would see the others at church in the morning. We went home. And we did not just sleep. We rested in the promises of God and the yeses of Heaven. Sunday morning came early, especially after a long night. We walked into the church and made our way to sit next to my new friend Alicia and her family, which happened to be on the second row. Moments after worship started, Leora walked up to me and said, "Hey girl. Would you like to hold my baby?" I was so excited to say yes to her that I was not even sure that I spoke. We often peg men as being unintentional and forgetful, but not only did Eli remember that I wanted to hold his baby girl, but he was intentional in making sure that it happened. I cuddled and prayed over that sweet baby girl all throughout worship. As I was holding the baby, Leora went to the altar and started to worship. I could be wrong, but it felt like I was doing more than holding a baby girl. It felt like God was making a way for me to get something that I wanted while making sure that sweet Leora was able to take a few moments to meet with the King, which does not often happen when you are a mama to littles. As she worshipped at the altar, floods of youth surrounded her. Worshiping. Weeping. Praying. It was like a revival was breaking out, and we were all watching, taking part in it in real time. It was unlike anything I have experienced, truly. After the service, it was confirmed by Brenno that youth worshiping at the altar like that had NEVER happened. We were shocked and amazed to have experienced something so powerful.

Moving forward, after church, Brenno's family cooked lunch for us before sending us on our (almost) six-hour journey home. The lunch, the community, the conversation—it was life-giving. I did not want to leave; I literally looked up houses on Zillow on the way home to see if we could move to that area. Okay, I didn't really want to move there, but the way that group of people loved and served us without knowing us was unlike anything I had EVER experienced before. I grew up in church, and I was still in awe of their hospitality. As we drove home and I began to process all of the things that happened that weekend, I began to weep. From the time we walked into that Airbnb to the time we left Brenno's family home, it was like God was saying, "Kayleigh, I see you." When we walked into that Airbnb and were met with anniversary gifts, it was like God was saying, "I know your marriage has been hard. But I see you." When we went to the church and we sat in on that "youth leader" small group, and then Donovan vouched for me to be on the panel, it was like God said, "Kayleigh, I am aware of your desire to lead people. And I know you feel called to preach. None of your wants or needs have fallen on deaf ears." When we sat at Applebee's and Miles prophesied healing over Donovan, it was like God was saying, "Kayleigh, I hear your prayers and your requests for healing for your husband. The answer is on the way." When

Leora brought me her baby, it was like I heard the whisper of God, "Kayleigh, I know you want kids. I saw you lose the boys. I will give you kids that a system cannot take." And, as I sat at Brenno's family home building community with some of the most genuine people I have ever met, it was like I heard God saying, "Kayleigh, I know you desire a community like this. I will bring it."

All at once, in one weekend, I felt so seen by God. Every detail of my life that I thought He did not care about, He responded to. All at once. And just like that, after two years tucked away in a cleft that felt like a prison cell, I was finally free.

EPILOGUE

When the boys lived with us, at the height of COVID-19, Disney released their movie *Frozen 2* on Disney Plus. In one of the first few scenes of the movie, Elsa sings a song titled *Into the Unknown*. The lyrics say, "I've had my adventure, I don't need something new. I am afraid of what I'm risking if I follow you into the unknown." If I had to sum this book up into a small run-on sentence, I would use those lyrics. For many years of my life, I had taken on all of the adventures I could handle. I experienced the adventure of children, church hurt, marriage, a pandemic, having (literally) zero dollars, and ministry losses. Every single adventure left me physically weeping, spiritually depleted, and just so worn down.

I had convinced myself in the midst of every hurt that I did not want to move forward into the things that I knew God was calling me to because I "had had enough adventure" and I "didn't need anything new." I was "afraid of what I would risk" if I followed God into the unknown. Would my future be met with more heartbreak, more tears, and more battle wounds that never seemed to heal completely before I was struck again?

At the end of Elsa's song, she says, "Don't you know there's part of me that loves to go into the unknown?" Despite every fear and every battle wound, I am a Christ follower. Even though at many times my humanity desires to stay stagnant, my spirit man deeply desires to go where Christ is leading—into the unknown. I have spent the last several months walking through uncharted—at least for me—territory. Between cancer, book writing and publishing, and starting a podcast, the list of the unknowns that I have stepped into gets longer almost daily. I won't lie; the unknown is scary. It is frightening to step into your future, wondering if God is going to meet you there. But there is so much peace in knowing that I am taking the steps to become who God has created me to be.

One last thought I want to add is not my thoughts, but it is the scripture that can be found in Proverbs 13:12. This scripture says, "Hope deferred makes the heart sick, but a longing fulfilled is a tree of life." For many years, my hope was deferred and my heart was sick as a result. Maybe you can relate to that. But a longing fulfilled is a tree of life. I cannot tell you today as I wrap up this book that every desire and longing I have is fulfilled, but I can tell you that I am resting in the arms of Jesus as I fight alongside my husband for his healing, we are asking the questions about what fertility looks like after chemotherapy, we are stepping into greater ministry opportunities and learning to navigate these opportunities together. I am not sure that all of my longings will ever be fulfilled until I reach Heaven, but I am certain that my hope is not deferred. It is 100% in Jesus, and I am finding peace, comfort, and rest that I am becoming her.